WHEN THE DISCIPLE COMES OF AGE

Christian Identity in the Twenty-First Century

Diarmuid O'Murchu, MSC

ORBIS BOOKS
www.orbisbooks.com

ORBIS BOOKS
www.orbisbooks.com

Fathers and Brothers
MARYKNOLL™

Founded in 1970, Orbis Books endeavors to publish works that enlighten the mind, nourish the spirit, and challenge the conscience. The publishing arm of the Maryknoll Fathers and Brothers, Orbis seeks to explore the global dimensions of the Christian faith and mission, to invite dialogue with diverse cultures and religious traditions, and to serve the cause of reconciliation and peace. The books published reflect the views of their authors and do not represent the official position of the Maryknoll Society. To learn more about Maryknoll and Orbis Books, please visit our website at www.maryknollsociety.org.

Copyright © 2019 by Diarmuid O'Murchu

Published by Orbis Books, Box 302, Maryknoll, NY 10545-0302.

All rights reserved.

No part of this publication may be reproduced or transmitted in any form or by any means, electronic or mechanical, including photocopying, recording, or any information storage or retrieval system, without prior permission in writing from the publisher.

Queries regarding rights and permissions should be addressed to: Orbis Books, P.O. Box 302, Maryknoll, NY 10545-0302.

Manufactured in the United States of America

Library of Congress Cataloging-in-Publication Data

Names: O'Murchu, Diarmuid, author.
Title: When the disciple comes of age : Christian identity in the twenty-first century / by Diarmuid O'Murchu.
Description: Maryknoll : Orbis Books, 2019. | Includes bibliographical references and index.
Identifiers: LCCN 2019008906 (print) | LCCN 2019022174 (ebook) ISBN 9781626983373 (pbk.)
Subjects: LCSH: Spiritual formation. | Christianity—21st century. | Identification (Religion) | Identity (Psychology)—Religious aspects—Christianity.
Classification: LCC BV4511 .O23 2019 (print) | LCC BV4511 (ebook) | DDC 270.8/3—dc23
LC record available at https://lccn.loc.gov/20 19008906
LC ebook record available at https://lccn.loc.gov/2019022174

Contents

Introduction

Indian spiritual wisdom, ancient and modern, highlights the role of the guru in the achievement of spiritual maturity. It is a distinctively male construct, clearly rooted in the patriarchal bias that characterizes all the great world religions. The guru (who tends to be male) is depicted as the adult teacher, and the disciple as the learning child—hence the frequently cited adage: when the disciple is ready, the guru will appear.

But what happens in the evolving culture of the twenty-first century when we find growing numbers of people achieving spiritual maturity and transcending the traditional frame of teacher and pupil, or guru and disciple. A paradigm shift seems to be at work here, a kind of reversal of roles that for many is strange and bewildering. The emerging axiom sounds quite different: *when the disciple comes of age, the guru must disappear!*

In the contemporary world, the disappearance of the guru tends to be perceived in either the rejection (or transcendence) of religious authority, or the option to abandon religion entirely. Within a Buddhist context, including many attracted to Buddhist meditation practices, the disappearance of the guru tends to be heard in rather individualistic terms, denoting a new quality of spiritual self-assurance, in which devotees work things out for themselves. This may indicate an adult coming-of-age in terms of religious maturity, but it can also morph into a self-inflated idolatry characteristic of several strands of fundamentalist religion, or worse still, it can feed the exaggerated individualism of our time.

For the present work I adopt the title for an autobiographical analysis of my own faith journey as a Christian, and to provide a kind of launching pad for the evolving Christian wisdom unfolding throughout the opening decades of the twenty-first century. The autobiographical material is likely to parallel that of many adult faith-seekers I have come to know over the past forty years, in a movement broadly known as *progressive Christianity*. I trust that by sharing my own experiences of growth and engagement of new horizons I will be affirming and further encouraging those traversing this pilgrim journey in the evolutionary context of our time.

The second goal in writing this book is considerably more complex and ambitious. As a social scientist I detect substantial upheavals in the understanding and appropriation of Christian faith today. At times, it feels like all the time-sanctioned foundations of truth and certainty are imploding due to fatigue or irrelevance. Our inherited patriarchal certainties, and the accompanying power games—along with the codependency that they instill in believers—seem to be lying in ruins. The evolutionary context of the twenty-first century requires something very different. To date, what that novel emergence will look like is unknown. For growing numbers of spiritual seekers, especially those of older years, investing energy in the inherited package simply does not make sense. Something new is emerging that exerts a far stronger appeal, and that appeal often arises from somewhere deep within our searching hearts.

This brief outline sounds very polarized: the old is so deficient it is not worth retaining, while the new offers enormous hope, despite the fact that those aspiring for it have little tangible evidence for what it means in practical terms. As a social scientist I am heavily committed to the work of integration. In more traditional lingo, I believe in *reworking the tradition*, not simply retrieving or revitalizing the past, but mobilizing the enduring wisdom of tradition so that it also empowers us for the evolving future. As an evolutionist I believe we are enveloped in an empowering story that outstretches all our human and academic constructs, including the binary opposites of past and future. As an organic earth species we are forever recycling the sources of wisdom, including our spiritual hopes and aspirations.

I do believe and accept that Jesus of Nazareth is a historical person, and I am reasonably well acquainted with the research into his historical significance. Yet the older I get, the more I am convinced that, for me as a Christian, Jesus holds an archetypal significance that opens up other transhistorical dimensions of faith, eminently significant for the twenty-first century. It is immensely encouraging to see that several Christian scholars—and thousands (perhaps millions) of Christians—are reimagining their faith along these lines. At times it feels immensely exciting and empowering, admittedly leaving one with several daunting challenges on how to bring this faith into engagement with the several dysfunctional and oppressive elements of modern life. And what can be particularly discouraging is the inertia and irrelevance evidenced in so many Christian churches; not surprisingly, many people move out of churches, not so much in terms of rejection, but to honor a sense of wanting to move further ahead.

The present book revisits the Christian story, embracing many of the empowering insights surfacing in contemporary research. My target audience is that of wise elders, a small but growing cohort, which, I suspect, will be critical catalysts in the evolving Christian faith of the twenty-first century. While our modern world tends to dismiss the elderly as unproductive and burdensome, I envisage a future elder culture with enormous evolutionary potential. Our world is growing rapidly older, with those of more advanced years playing central roles in almost every sphere of public life. Counterintuitively, I suspect they will be in the vanguard for Christian prophetic witness as we move deeper into the twenty-first century.

In Adult Faith Development, we seek to build on experience, both personal and transpersonal. From the rich reservoir of lived experience, we make deeper connections with the beliefs we have inherited from "revealed" truth; revelation becomes an ongoing, unfolding process of mutual learning and interpersonal enrichment. My strategy, therefore, throughout this book is to combine personal narrative with the evolving intellectual wisdom of the twenty-first century. I focus on *intellect* as an endowment we all share, rather than academic status, an attainment of a relatively small sector of global humanity. While I cherish the inherited wisdom of the learned, and invoke scholarly wisdom throughout the present work, I want to build upon the wisdom of the human heart informed by the evolutionary momentum of our time.

Part One

Setting the Scene

Our postmodern era is often perceived as a time of reckless liberalism and rampant individualism. Trust in inherited, conventional wisdom is quite low, and formal authorities in all walks of life command decreasing levels of respect and credibility. And in the ensuing confusing fluidity, we detect what might best be described as a panic reaction, predominantly from people of younger years.

This reactionary fundamentalism, perceptible in politics and religion, desires security, simplicity, and certainty. For those who hold this view the world has become so unsafe that at times they feel overwhelmed by the waves of change. They would like to halt the stampede and, in the process of trying, often seek a return to the perceived security and stability of bygone days.

With postmodern folk seeking greater freedom (at any price), and the petrified minority trying to return life to some sense of normalcy, media are often lured into the sensationalism that emerges from the clash of ideologies. Here we run the great danger of missing the deeper, discerning truth—namely, the evolutionary optic, which provides a more focused context in which to understand what is happening within and around us.

Part One of this book delineates the broad contours of this evolutionary shift. Every evolutionary epoch evokes new horizons that are both promising and perilous. Such epochs are dislocating for everybody, but some handle things better than others. Evolution has a kind of momentum of its own, often quite different from the predictable dynamics identified by the neo-Darwinians. Evolutionary awakenings tend to beget strange attractors, and these can provide crucial clues into what is luring us into a new future.

One such attractor is the *coming-of-age*, explored in the present work. In the human community it is the largely unrecognized upsurge of human gentrification. Our aging human population marks an evolutionary—and revolutionary—coming-of-age for which few cultures or nations are prepared. Its meaning defies so much rational discourse and patriarchal control. To make some sense of what is transpiring, we need an alternative wisdom—what I've described as *the archetypal*.

We are being lured into an enlarged horizon, where several previous cultural constructs are no longer sustainable. The coevolution of person and planet evokes several mega-adjustments—to our economics, politics, social policies, and religions. We need a multidisciplinary wisdom, much talked about in recent times but seldom adopted in our social, political, or religious analyses. And we need to outgrow the dualistic splitting that has kept the spiritual and the secular at loggerheads for far too long.

These are just some of the transitional challenges evoking a new coming-of-age—for person and planet alike.

1

Coming of Age

What Is at Stake?

When I was a child, I spoke like a child, I thought like a child, I reasoned like a child; when I became an adult, I gave up childish ways.

—St. Paul (1 Cor. 13:11)

I become who I will be within the network of relations, rooted in the non-human, blooming in the intimate, branching into the unknown.

—Catherine Keller

Coming-of-age is a phrase widely used to denote the shift toward adult maturity, particularly the evolution from adolescence into young adulthood. Traditionally this shift was marked in several indigenous cultures by a rite of passage, highlighting a readiness for more adult responsibilities related to the life and welfare of the group. In indigenous cultures, there is often also a more subtle dimension, as the initiate is entrusted with novel responsibilities for the care and nurturance of the earth. Becoming an adult also denotes engagement with a greater sense of complexity, an invitation to become a more mature and creative earthling.

3

Embracing adult maturity has long been viewed as a human endeavor belonging primarily to human persons in their anthropological and cultural contexts. The present work seeks to extend the horizon of such growth to include transpersonal dimensions of universe and planet—indeed, the entire scope of God's creation. No longer can human aspiration, meaning, or potential be understood over against the natural world. We are earthlings, with hearts, minds, and even brains programmed for cosmic interconnectedness. The maturity and integrity of our coming-of-age in the twenty-first century depend largely on how we engage and internalize these more expansive horizons.

Human Development in the Twentieth Century

First, however, let's review the developmental research on human growth toward maturity as it unfolded in the latter half of the twentieth century. In Western cultures, adult maturity has long been marked by features such as the ability to open a bank account, drive a public vehicle, and cast a vote for government; more importantly, it is characterized by embracing study or training that equips a person for the responsibilities of adult life.

Coming-of-age also denotes a developmental shift from the exploratory nature of adolescence to an expectation of settling down so that one can prepare effectively for meaningful employment (in order to earn good money), and for the relational responsibilities that will be involved in marriage, setting up a home, and begetting a family.

It sounds predictable, neat, and efficient, and is presumed to make for good citizenship as well as personal growth and economic progress. It was very much the cultural norm until the mid-twentieth century, and then everything changed so rapidly that many felt as if society itself were falling apart. Coming-of-age no longer felt like an appropriate description, and as we move into the twenty-first century the term is loaded with even greater ambiguity.

We note across most modern cultures an extension of the developmental phase known as adolescence. Teenage years are widely associated with rebellion and reaction, insecurity and exploration, and belligerent behavior that gradually gives way to the more levelheaded engagement associated with adult maturity. But this is no longer a predictable or linear process, nor does it run its course by our late teenage years. What one time was considered a typical adolescent reaction can now be observed in people throughout their twenties, and in several cases right into the early thirties.

For many developmental psychologists today, emerging adulthood (as it is now called) is deemed to be one of the most precarious of the life stages, characterized by self-doubt and anxiety, ambivalence around life values, and fear and apprehension of decision-making. Several factors contribute to this prolonged restlessness, three of which can clearly be observed:

- *Living in a culture of mass information.* While many young adults seem to ride the wave of the new information tectonics, the stress of the daily demand to be visible, connected, and popular—to adopt to the ever more seductively salacious fashions and become adept at being a multitasker—take an emotional toll that thus far has not been extensively researched. The alarming rates of suicide among young adults, the fluidity and unpredictability of intimate relating, and a worldwide drug-abuse problem are just a few of the symptoms suggesting that all is not well with our emerging adults.
- *Our fluid work-ethic.* The notion of a job for life, with the securities that accompany it, is largely a legacy of the past. Contract labor, with its short-term prospects, the continuous demand to be on the lookout for the next piece of work, and the financial instabilities that ensue, also carry a heavy psychological toll on emerging adults.

- *Relational fluidity*. While some religions still seek to uphold the monogamous heterosexual mode of human intimacy, and the hope of permanent marriage, home, and children, this inherited ideal is rapidly being consigned to the archives of history. In several European countries cohabitation is extensively practiced. The emergence of the LGBT phenomenon is not merely about the acceptance of diverse sexual orientation. It marks a radical departure from the conventional psychosexual culture of the past, leaving many young adults today unsure of their psychosexual uniqueness and gender identity, and trying to make sense of a relational landscape that is now highly fluid and unpredictable.

In developmental psychology, the mid-life stage (roughly ages thirty-five to fifty) was a hot topic of the 1970s and 1980s. It still remains a time of significant growth and transformation, now widely regarded as the stage during which we come to terms with what adulthood really means, letting go of the several cultural lures of achievement and power, and looking within rather than without for the true value of self and others. With more extensive availability of counseling and therapy, and a vast range of mutually supportive networks, mid-lifers realize more readily the pitfalls of a second adolescence and the hankering after the forever-stay-young allurement that seductive advertising promotes.

Classifying Our Elders

The study of life stages, initially pioneered by the German American psychologist Erik Erikson (d. 1994), devoted considerable attention to the early foundational growth of childhood up to the stage of puberty. The character formation of those early years was believed to be foundational for all that would transpire throughout the rest of our lives. For the greater part, character was set by late adolescence and could not be significantly altered thereafter. Moreover, the older we became, the more difficult it would be to change attitudes, outlooks, and personal behavior.

In the latter half of the twentieth century, that linear progressive view fell into disfavor. Developmental psychologists acknowledged a much more complex trajectory, with the childhood foundations carrying enduring significance, but capable of being reworked and integrated anew throughout the entire life span. Even in old age, change and new adaptation could take place; more significantly, the new quality of creativity that evolved with the wisdom of older years captivated the attention of a new generation of researchers and is of special interest for the present work.

When the American developmental psychologist James Fowler (1981) first outlined his stages of faith development, he moved from consideration of mid-lifers straight into his treatment of the elderly, postulating the universalizing stage attained by the rare few as a possibility for anybody from forty-five years of age onward. Other researchers, notably Susanne Cook-Greuter (1994; 1999), Gail Sheehy (1995), Bill Plotkin (2008), and Kenneth Stokes (1982), provide a more refined analysis of this final stage. Plotkin divides it into two stages (early and late elderhood), as I do in my own earlier research (see O'Murchu 2010; 2014b).

In the closing decades of the twentieth century, many people were offered the option of early retirement (from age fifty-five onward), and since many of these people were still healthy and active in every sense, opportunities were sought to reemploy their talents and resources. One significant outcome of this emergence was the University of the Third Age (popularly known as UTA or U3A). Today this educational facility, reserved to the over-fifties, accommodates an estimated 10 million people in the Americas, Europe, Australia, India, and China. The popular prejudicial perception of older people being unemployable, nonproductive, and a drain on financial and health resources quickly changed, although much awareness-raising still needs to be done.

Beyond early retirement (fifty-five-plus), a further life stage requires renewed attention, namely those over the age of seventy.

In religious terms this subgroup is assumed to be in declining health and are thus admonished to do penance and prepare to meet God in death and judgment. In the Hindu faith, the elderly devotee is even encouraged to leave home and family, and assume a life of greater austerity and simplicity, for example, *vanaprastha* (forest recluse) and *sanyasi* (complete renunciation).

In the 1970s, a revitalization of the notion of the wise elder came to the fore, with Fowler's characteristic of *universality* evoking the attention of various researchers. Despite its scholarly limitations, the pioneering work of James Fowler (1981) still remains seminal. Initially a Western development, it has now become much more widespread, with implications for the global consciousness of our time and particularly its spiritual (mystical) implications (comprehensively reviewed in the *Journal of Religious Gerontology*, initially launched in 1984).

Two critical factors come into play here. The first, already noted, is what Theodore Roszak (2001) calls *the longevity revolution*, with those of older age becoming not merely numerically stronger in population terms but also a determining political and economic force, as I indicate shortly. Second, the information explosion has had, and will continue to have, a major influence, not merely on our emerging adults but also on these older people. While they don't exhibit the multitech dexterity of the young nor their fascination with modern information technology, they imbibe the newly emerging consciousness for *interconnectedness*, *wholeness*, and *universality*, for which James Gollnick employs the term *gerotranscendence* (Gollnick 2008, 223). They become curious and eager to learn more; their intuition is freshly awakened, and their imaginations are stretched in the direction of expansion and universality, characteristics of consciousness in our time with some significant theological implications, as illustrated by Australian theologian Anthony J. Kelly (2015).

Unfortunately, because our dominant culture is so antiaging (except for the technological compulsion toward perpetual youthfulness and the end of dying) and largely dismissive of the elderly as useless and nonproductive, only limited research has gone into the alternative phenomenon I am highlighting. I know from personal experience that an alternative elder culture is arising (rapidly and universally), and that in a matter of a few decades it will exert substantial influence on our global value systems.

We are rapidly approaching the critical threshold when in several Western countries the elderly will become (1) the dominant voters, much more critically aware of political policies, and not easily lured to support the inherited party system; and (2) the dominant purchasers, whose buying options will not be determined by popular fashion or commercial spin, but by aesthetic, ecological, and more responsible values. Thanks to the preponderance of these older consumers, sustainability in values and practices is likely to expand significantly, requiring major changes in marketing, advertising, and consumer practice, the demands consistently upheld by Democratic candidate Bernie Sanders in the run-up to the 2016 U.S. presidential election.

❈

Personal Reflection

Some years ago about a hundred people turned up for a public lecture at the London School of Economics. Theodore Roszak, professor of cultural history at the University of California at Berkeley (d. 2011), was in town addressing the vision outlined in his latest book, The Making of an Elder Culture *(Roszak 2009). Several years earlier I had read what was to become his best-known work,* The Making of a Counter Culture *(1969), followed in 1979 by a lesser-known work,* Person/Planet, *which also struck deep resonances for me. Ever since I first read Roszak back in the 1970s, I detected a maverick of prophetic significance.*

Despite my admiration for Roszak, I found myself having other reactions as the public lecture unfolded. His initial enthusiasm about the vast potential of a world growing older did not sit comfortably with me. However, as Roszak continued to speak I began to realize that my own prejudice and fear were inhibiting my receptivity. I realized I had to listen more attentively, and then I began to detect the several nuances embedded in his counterintuitive claim that the future of humanity rested not with our younger people but with our wise elders.

In the informal conversations after the lecture, I learned that virtually everybody present had a similar set of reactions: from initial incredulity, to the suspicion that there might be some truth in what he was saying, to the eventual realization that in all probability his insights were probably spot on.

Over the past forty years I have had the privilege of working with many people of older years. Most of my workshop and seminar attendees tend to be over seventy years of age. They themselves often bemoan the fact that young people are not present to share in the unfolding wisdom. Consistently I find myself wondering if young people could absorb and internalize the evolving wisdom of our time. And I often explicitly ask: is this not a wisdom that requires the maturation and life experience of our wise elders?

Paradoxical though it may sound, in a world where old age is viewed so negatively and so dismissively, I perceive growing cultural and sociological evidence to support the view that as older people become more numerous and visible on our earth, and give more overt expression to their sustainable lifestyles and spiritual values, they are likely to become the cultural catalysts for more wholesome and empowering ways of being. It would not be the first time in history in which the survival of the fittest has morphed into a set of outcomes that few, if any, of us had foreseen.

❄

My interest in this new subgroup is mainly spiritual and religious in nature. They are already redefining several aspects of Christian faith. These elders (whom I define as fifty-five and older) come mainly from a formal religious background, tend to be well-educated, and often belong to the middle to the upper classes. However, they question almost everything in their inherited faith and wish to stretch spiritual understandings far beyond conventional religious belief. They fit perfectly Pitirim Sorokin's notion of the "restless middle classes" for whom sacredness is universal and predates religion. In Sorokin's analysis, these people are the primary catalysts of evolutionary change (more in Sorokin 1950). And in their expansive vision they seek to outgrow the dualistic split between the sacred and the secular.

Coming-of-Age in a Postmodern World

Thus far, I am describing *coming-of-age* within the chronological developmental framework adopted by several psychologists over the past one hundred years. The reader can readily note my specialized interest in the older life stages and the unique contributions that wise elders are likely to make as we move deeper into the twenty-first century. However, the coming-of-age explored throughout this book carries a range of other meanings, and together these lead to a fresh description of archetypal truth, particularly in part 2 of this book. Among the other features denoted by the notion of coming-of-age, I consider the following to be particularly significant:

- The postmodern worldview, which seeks to transcend the narrow totalizing ideologies of patriarchal cultures: one God, one power, one truth, one absolute. Learning to live creatively with a range of new cultural fluidities requires levels of adult maturity unknown in previous times.
- New scientific breakthroughs such as relativity theory and quantum physics, transcending the narrower mechanistic, rationalistic paradigms of the past two thousand years.

- The new cosmological horizon, within which the figure of 13.8 billion years has become almost a household term of reference.

- Less widely known, and likely to be of substantial import throughout the twenty-first century, is the expanded human story of some 7 million years (more in O'Murchu 2008). We begin to understand our human role in creation in a vastly expanded horizon with substantial implications for how we function in the world.

- Extensive travel and cross-cultural exposures challenging us to outgrow narrow nationalistic, ethnic, and religious identities.

- For faith development, and particularly for Christian belief as outlined in part 2 herein, we witness a new adult criticality whereby people either abandon traditional faith or seek out alternatives open to adult engagement and participation (more in Gollnick 2008).

These are just some of the twentieth- and twenty-first-century evolutionary developments that beget a new coming-of-age, moving us out of narrow ideological constraints into broader, diverse modes of understanding and engagement. However, all such developments coexist with what might be called *shadow resistances*. We see a highly amorphous spiritual awakening with a diverse range of expressions, paralleled by a global increase in rigid religious fundamentalism. Globalization, while undermining the power monopoly of the nation-state, has created new political and economic monstrosities of even greater totalizing impact. A nonviolent consciousness promoted by several peace-and-justice initiatives has not diminished the frequency of warfare, violence, and a highly lucrative arms trade. In traditional Jungian language, light and shadow sit side by side.

Nonetheless, the coming-of-age that I am describing is an *evolutionary imperative* of our time, with long-term benefits that will not be reversed. Like all evolutionary breakthroughs, the transformation will be primarily for those at the ready, and that tends to be a minority. The majority will respond with business-as-usual, with another minority reacting negatively. In time, however, evolutionary breakthroughs become culturally normalized, as with the current globalization of information accessibility.

Return to the Wise Elder

Every culture looks to its youth as the prospective hope of the future, the ones who hopefully will carry forward the inherited wisdom of the past and carve out new furrows for future growth and progress. This perception made sense in cultures where progress was viewed in more linear terms, within which leading institutions changed little over long periods of time.

Ours is a different time. We are witnessing transformative leaps of quantum possibility, the likes of which we have not been seen for several centuries. It takes the discerning wisdom of age and maturity—first to read what is transpiring, and then to determine how best to appropriate and internalize the new evolutionary momentum.

I don't think young people will be the primary catalysts of this new future. As indicated above, we see young adults struggling to make ends meet, to make sense of a world of bewildering choices and a pace of life in which many feel like losers. Survival, rather than flourishing, is the primary preoccupation of our younger members.

Our older members will exhibit the resilience and wisdom to hold their nerves and help us all to make sense of what is happening. Spared the daily burden of paying off a mortgage, rearing a family, and holding down a job, the elders are free for the quality of engagement needed at this evolutionary time. And many among this age cohort have appropriated the multidisciplinary wisdom necessary for the integration that is involved. Moreover, many have transcended the deadly dualistic split between the sacred and the secular, and thus are capable of being more discerning in reading what is going on and better able to choose proactive lines of action.

The dominant culture will not likely change its perceptions of our older members as being an economic burden, a social lethargy, a cultural irrelevancy. Preoccupied as we are with agile, functional consumers and producers, we are unlikely to read in a discerning way the upsurge of a new evolutionary threshold, begetting a different future for all of us. In chapter 3, I outline the feel and tenor of this emerging evolutionary narrative. Meanwhile, I want to review the breakdown we are going through, what meaning we might detect in its fragmentation, and how we can let go of that which sustained us so well for so long.

If we want to be part of the new, we need to learn the subtle wisdom of what it means to die to the old. The Enlightenment cherished its patriarchal gurus. Everybody looked to those at the top, perceived to be endowed with superior wisdom, and assumed to be blessed with something of the divine knowledge from on high.

But who believes that anymore? A hermeneutic of suspicion permeates every sphere of life today. The sources for long-cherished wisdom seem weary and exhausted. They fail to satisfy the search for something much deeper, a knowledge that enables us to make sense of the rapidly evolving world of our time and show us how to engage in a proactive and empowering way.

This desire for a new integration is the coming-of-age I seek to explore in the pages of this book. Characterized on the one hand by disillusionment and rejection of the past, it also embodies a passionate desire for a new and better world. On closer observation—what I later describe as the art of discernment—we are not dealing with a simplistic and reckless abandonment of all that has gone before. What we are rejecting are the dogmatized edifices whereby a onetime truth claimed that it was permanent and could never be altered. That is alien to the evolutionary trust that informs contemporary humans within and without. The coming-of-age characterizing our time has integration as its ultimate goal. The desired outcome is not another dualistic split between past and present, but a new synthesis seeking to integrate and celebrate all that is sacred within the canopy of universal life.

2

The Disappearing Guru

And What Then?

*Is there anything more dangerous than dissatisfied and
irresponsible Gods who don't know what they want?*
—Yuval Noah Harari

*Indeed, if we are to claim some kind of continuity—as
Christian reading surely must—it is a continuity that is
deeply hidden and endlessly problematic.*
—Walter Brueggemann

A range of Eastern meditation and spiritual practices infiltrated
the West throughout the 1960s and 1970s. Largely in reaction
to staid, legalistic religion, millions opted for the refreshing
awakening of something quite different—more person-centered,
joy-filled, and promising new liberation from the strains and
stresses of life. Everybody could learn the new techniques, and it
seems millions did. Gurus like Maharishi Mahesh Yogi (of TM
fame), Swami A. C. Bhaktivedanta Prabhupada (of Hare Krishna
renown), Bhagwan Shree Rajneesh (founder of the Rajneesh
movement), and Swami Satchidananda (Integral Yoga) became

household names in the United States and drew huge crowds of followers. By the end of the century, however, the nine-day wonders had waned considerably, and some of the gurus themselves had fallen into disrepute.

A type of cultic codependency began to take its toll. Many people had submitted to the new gurus like they had to the old religious authorities. It was an amalgam fraught with pitfalls, particularly the naiveté of the followers and the power games of the gurus themselves. Central to many of those developments was a sense of trust in the guru that carried some dangerous elements of patriarchal codependency. Statements like, "When the disciple is ready, the guru will appear," or "To forsake the guru and his ideals is to spurn the help sent by God," convey a deceptive, collusive ploy that many devotees did not detect.

Ken Wilber, himself often upheld as a guru, offers valuable advice on how to handle in a healthier and more mature way the disciple-guru relationship. Particularly important is the need to recognize when a level of enlightenment has been attained, indicating that the disciple needs to move on and thus changing, or even outgrowing, the dependence on the guru. The guru's authority is a temporary phase (cf. Wilber et al. 1987, 257, 249). Several schools of psychotherapy are also aware of such transitional movement and encourage clients to consider moving into various support groups where they can develop more interdependent skills and avail themselves of more communal resources.

American counselor and psychotherapist Gregory C. Bogart (1992) addresses the process of how a disciple can—and should—separate from a guru-type spiritual guide. From his reflections I adopt the adage upon which this book is built: *When the disciple comes of age, the guru must disappear.* The coming-of-age examined in this book is not postulated on a parent-child relationship but rather on that of mutual adults whose formative relationships belong to a different organic context. Equality, mutuality, and collaboration are among the central dynamics. The ensuing growth is interdependent and mutually empowering, transcending the directive dependency frequently adopted in past religious and spiritual formation.

Postpatriarchal Narratives

I open this chapter with two narratives illustrating the stubborn endurance of patriarchal domination. These stories serve as contemporary parables on the demise of the disappearing guru, while also presenting alternatives for more egalitarian empowering possibilities. First I introduce the 2017 British biographical movie *Victoria & Abdul*, directed by Stephen Frears and written by Lee Hall. The film is based on the book of the same name by Shrabani Basu, about the real-life relationship between Queen Victoria of the United Kingdom and her Indian Muslim servant, Abdul Karim. Karim, a young prison clerk from Agra, India, is instructed to travel to England for Queen Victoria's Golden Jubilee in 1887 to present her with a *mohur*, a gold coin that has been minted as a token of appreciation and gratitude from British-ruled India.

The queen, who is lonely and tired of her fawning courtiers, develops a personal interest in, and later a unique friendship with, Abdul. She spends time with him alone and promotes him to become her *Munshi* (teacher). She asks him to teach her Urdu and the Qur'an. When Victoria discovers that he is married, she invites his wife and mother-in-law to join him in England.

Victoria treats Abdul as a son, something that confuses and baffles her entire household, including her son Bertie, the prime minister of the time. Various members of the household plot to undermine their relationship, hoping that Abdul will be sent home, but he manages to stay until her death in 1901, when he then has to face the resentment and wrath of those whose "power" felt so threatened by this charming and harmless young man.

The movie serves as a kind of parable of what is likely to unfold when the guru must disappear, now that the disciple has come of age. In a sense the old queen Victoria came of age, reclaiming her sanity and humanity thanks to the transgression of

young Abdul and his warm, reassuring personality. But the powerful courtiers were dreading the consequences of the "disappearing
guru." They just could not handle a woman who became more
of a human person rather than a mere bureaucratic queen. And
no sooner was she dead than he was banished in an attempt to
restore bureaucratic balance to the royal domain.

A second exemplary story is that of a female German math-
ematician, Amalie Emmy Noether (1882–1935), who lived at a
time when girls were not allowed to attend college to follow an
academic career. Nonetheless, she was admitted to a general "fin-
ishing school," and in 1900 was certified to teach English and
French. But rather than teaching, she pursued a university education in her favored subject, mathematics. Despite formidable
opposition she eventually received her mathematics PhD in 1907.

Noether worked at the Mathematical Institute of Erlangen,
without pay or title, from 1908 to 1915. In 1915 she joined the
Mathematical Institute in Göttingen and started working with
Felix Klein and David Hilbert on Einstein's general theory of
relativity. In 1918 she proved two theorems that were basic for
both general relativity and elementary particle physics. One is still
known as "Noether's Theorem."

But she still could not join the faculty at Göttingen University because of her gender. Noether was only allowed to lecture
under Hilbert's name, as his assistant. Hilbert and Albert Einstein interceded for her, and in 1919 she obtained permission
to lecture, although still without a salary. In 1922 she became
an "associate professor without tenure" and began to receive a
small salary. Her status did not change while she remained at
Göttingen, owing not only to prejudices against women but also
because she was a Jew, a Social Democrat, and a pacifist.

Emmy Noether made many contributions to the field of
mathematics. She spent her time studying abstract algebra, with
special attention to rings, groups, and fields. Because of her unique
insights, she was able to see relationships that traditional algebra
experts failed to discern. She didn't merely represent a feminist

perspective in a male-dominated world but paved the way for the archetypal coming-of-age being explored in the present work.

The Disappearing Guru

The French Revolution is often considered to be the first major dent in the imperial mode of governance that had prevailed for the several previous centuries. Feudalism was destroyed. All privileged classes were abolished. Capitalism became the new economic system. Slavery was abolished in all French colonies. In 1792 all nonpropertied classes (workers, peasants, artisans) were given equal political rights. Social equality and socialism became popular ideas. Liberty, equality, and fraternity became the new progressive slogans.

However, colonial empire-building was still rampant throughout many parts of the world during the nineteenth and twentieth centuries; even the French joined in the international oppression. A more subtle and subversive toppling of power happened in the mid-twentieth century, from 1960 onward, and this is what augmented and boosted the metaphorical disappearance of the guru.

Five key features characterize this massive cultural shift:

1. *A rapidly emerging distrust of all patriarchal structures and institutions.* Power from the top, with the masculine urge for control and domination, lost a great deal of credibility. New-Agers opted out of national allegiances and sought a return to the simplicity of nature, within and beyond national boundaries. Religious deviants no longer felt guilty about challenging and abandoning long-held religious beliefs.

2. *Young people particularly began to travel internationally.* The rucksack is a powerful symbol of the 1960s. Nationalistic and religious monopolies lost much of their command on power and truth. In 1960 alone, seventeen African countries declared independence from Western colonialism.

3. *The stiff upper lip so symbolic of patriarchal power gave way to an amorphous overflow of free love, hedonistic practices, charismatic spirituality, and anarchic social process.* Rationality

gave way not so much to the irrational as to a whole new awakening of imagination, intuition, and the power of the feminine. Freedom was in the air, with a kind of recklessness that was to prove both promising and perilous.

4. With the gradual emergence of the information age—especially through the internet and mobile phone—*a new global interconnectedness came into being.* Human awareness took a massive leap in prominence. Intellectuals began to mistrust academics, and information long reserved to the few in charge could now be Googled, even by semi-illiterate people.

5. *Absolute truth lost virtually all sense of meaning in the sciences and in the religious domain.* Critics were quick to condemn this new age of relativism and postmodernity, but for the greater part, those same critics failed to see the erosion of bigotry, idolatry, and the masculine monopoly of truth.

It wasn't that the guru disappeared; he was dislodged. It was not a case of losing his power; he lost his credibility. The critics will rightly retort that he has not been replaced by anything more meaningful. We have inherited a paradigm shift that cannot be negotiated simply by replacing one regime with another. That is the patriarchal way of doing things. In a world of the quantum vacuum there is such an abundance of fullness, of so many unrealized possibilities, that we need a totally different wisdom to engage the vast range of creative possibilities, as illustrated by a modern scientist like Jude Currivan (2017). Our inherited patriarchal institutions don't know how to deal with this new evolutionary threshold. They have not yet come of age.

As a global family we are living through an unprecedented evolutionary shift. Governments and religions weary themselves trying to buffer us against the fallout. They ridicule and condemn the anarchic awakening. Many academics try to rationalize what is going on, adopting a range of elaborate philosophical and technical arguments, with postmodernism often the scapegoat. Religions are running scared, with Muslims building an ideological fortress that appeals to millions of frightened youths—hence the reason it is a rapidly growing religion, similar to fundamental sects in Christianity and in other major faiths.

Replacing the Guru

Generally speaking, evolution does not long tolerate a cultural vacuum. With the disappearance of the patriarchal guru, a new sense of authority came into play, and today can be observed on an international scale. John Feehan, onetime professor of microbiology in Ireland, now turned to exploring the interface of spirituality and contemporary science, provides this valuable overview of how the patriarchal guru is being replaced:

> When you are confronted by evidence that the faith in which you were brought up no longer provides an adequate explanation for the nature, meaning and purpose of your life, you have three choices. You can refuse to accept the evidence and continue as before. You can abandon the faith you grew up with, because it has proved to be inadequate. Or, third, you can accept the new knowledge and use it to develop a more mature understanding of what lies at the core of your beliefs. The first response is intellectually dishonest. The second is intellectual laziness. *The third is a stance of critical acceptance, leading to a reinterpretation of core concepts.* . . . It requires courage and a plethora of other virtues that have been gathering dust in your spirit. Every advance in understanding invites us into a deeper faith. (Feehan 2012, 148, emphasis added)

Personal Reflection

Shortly after I became a priest in the early 1970s, a local doctor asked to see me for a personal conversation. He informed me that he and his wife were using contraception (contrary to Catholic Church teaching), and he obviously felt disturbed in his conscience about the matter. He explained the extenuating circumstances in his marriage, whereby he and his wife felt they needed to use contraception. He was seeking guidance and advice.

I don't actually recall what I said to him. I remember being extremely tense. He being a medical doctor, and a married family man, I felt distinctly incompetent. I hope I offered some good pastoral attention, and I doubt if I gave any concrete advice.

Colleagues at the time informed me that a lot of conscientious Catholics, in the wake of the papal encyclical Humanae Vitae *(published in 1968), consulted priests when they found themselves in the kind of dilemma that the doctor had brought to me. Things began to change as we moved into the 1980s; a growing number of Catholics seemed to be coming of age and realized that it was not appropriate to be bringing such a dilemma to a priest. Instead, they began to frequent doctors and family planners. Within a further ten to fifteen years, another notable shift occurred: adults began to rely on each other's wisdom. A group of women meeting at the local nursery school conversed with each other about approaches to family planning; a group of men having an after-work social drink shared experiences and concerns around their "private lives." Couples having dinner together for a special occasion brought marital issues into their conversation. People had learned to trust the adult in each other.*

I use this Catholic example regarding family planning to illustrate not merely a remarkable coming-of-age but also to highlight the guru that was—and is—being dislodged. Initially people began to dispense with the religious guru. Shortly thereafter, they no longer felt a need to rely on the "professional" guru of doctor or family planner. It was not that people became arrogantly self-reliant. Many were not overtly critical either of priest or doctor. It was more a case of an awakening sense of adult maturity, with an accompanying realization that at the end of the day it was up to people themselves to deal more directly with the real concerns of their marital and familial situations.

❈

In this example the coming-of-age can clearly be discerned. Only on closer examination do we detect the disappearing guru and the emergence of an alternative sense of authoritative truth.

I trust the reader is getting the full weight of what is at stake in these reflections. Once more, let's recall the Buddhist-type aphorism upon which this book is based: *when the disciple comes of age, the guru must disappear.* The statement does not suggest that the guru must be changed, reformed, or renewed; something much more drastic is being suggested. I often encounter Catholics who dearly wish they could get leaders, such as priests or bishops, to see things differently; for many Catholics Pope Francis is often described as "a breath of fresh air," because he seems to be transcending the old-style authoritarianism so often associated with members of the Catholic hierarchy. Such observations are based on the hope of changing or reforming the guru. That is not what this book is about, particularly the material of the present chapter.

In the evolutionary context of the twenty-first century, we are trying to *get rid of* the inherited gurus, not change or reform them. As indicated above, we are not in pursuit of some new generation of gurus, but of a whole new way of discerning and accessing truth, aptly described by Scripture scholar Walter Brueggemann (2005) as *communal obedience.* Throughout this book I adopt a methodology that seeks to transcend both religious authority and the academic pursuit of truth. This is not about rejecting the past, with its long-honored claims on divinely informed authority. Rather it is an attempt to engage the evolutionary awakening of the twenty-first century in a more forthright and discerning way.

As already indicated, I am inspired by the prophetic vision of Scripture scholar Walter Brueggemann (2005), whose own search for more authentic veracity led him to pen these words:

But the Church, with its excessive penchant for dogmatic certitude, and the academy with its fascination with objective rationality, characteristically stop short of the evidence of *communal obedience*. . . . We will not claim again the authority of Scripture unless we recover its language, which is the language of trust and amazement, of gratitude and obedience. (9, 45, emphasis added)

The word *obedience* is derived from the Latin *obaudiere*, which means to listen attentively. Combined with the adjective *communal*, we begin to glean the evolving wisdom of our age, the discernment that engages the coming-of-age I am outlining in this book. It marks a distinctive cultural shift from individual guides, representing what has been perceived as a divinely informed authority, to a structure that will facilitate discerning truth and wisdom from the ground up.

So where is the continuity with the past, so essential for Christian theology on the one hand and for Darwinian evolution on the other? Our inherited understanding of evolution may be the major obstacle that needs more discerning attention. The theory of *punctuated equilibrium*, often associated with Neils Eldridge (1999), indicates that discontinuity is every bit as important as continuity in discerning evolutionary growth (or progress). New life, or breakthrough, often requires the death of what previously prevailed for something genuinely new to unfold. Additionally, we take on board the persuasive argument of John F. Haught (more in chapter 3 below) for whom *the lure of the future*, rather than the drive from the past, is the primary driving force in all evolutionary developments.

Traditionally we have clung to the past to a degree that is now proving to be stultifying and potentially destructive. Evolution is more complex than our patriarchal, controlling wisdom can admit. Truth is more amorphous and organic, and cannot be reduced to our anthropocentric linear mode of understanding.[1] We are living

---

[1] Worthy of note here is Walter Brueggemann's (2005) observation

through an era of epochal evolutionary shifts, in which many past truths are fading into history. Discontinuities abound, and truth is no longer in the hands or minds of the imperial gurus of the past. The art of consensus-making (outlined below) will prove a more reliable guide to the truth that illuminates our search and helps to set us free.

Some readers will be aware of these developments and undoubtedly can recall examples from their own lives of taking more personal and interpersonal initiatives than they would have done even a few decades ago. We also have to acknowledge, however, an equally strong counterdevelopment of fear and insecurity experienced by a growing minority of people. These are the young people who flock to sects, cults, and fundamentalist religions around the world, seeking a safe haven from the complexities of modern life, and in many cases regressing to a family-type womb where they can rely on others to guide, inform, and even make decisions for them. Although often associated with insecure younger people, this same sense of wanting a buffered existence is visible throughout several life stages.

The Art of Consensus-Making

In more secular language, we are exploring the art of consensus-making. In a world still gripped by dualistic splitting and adversarial debate, particularly in political and economic discourse, the move toward consensual discernment is both revolutionary and prophetic, echoing afresh the earlier notion of the *sensus fidelium/ fidei*.[2] Consensus is an agreement on the option that has the broadest

---

relating to the Christian Scriptures: "Indeed, if we are to claim some kind of continuity—as Christian reading surely must—it is a continuity that is *deeply hidden* and *endlessly problematic*" (152, emphasis in original).

[2] What is being highlighted here both includes and transcends the Catholic notion of the *sensus fidelium*. For several contemporary theologians, the notion of *sensus fidei/fidelium* is linked with the vision of the Second Vatican Council (1962–1965). Before the nineteenth century,

and strongest support, because all group members can live with it, *even if it is not the number-one choice for any particular member*. If each member feels that the others have listened, each may be willing to accept an option that is not their first choice, but is not opposed by anyone in the group. No one is asked to support an option they strongly oppose.

Consensus decision-making involves a collaborative discussion rather than an adversarial debate, and is therefore more likely to result in all parties reaching common ground. The benefits of consensus decision-making include:

- *Better decisions.* Because all perspectives in the group are taken into account, the resulting proposals can address all the concerns affecting the decision as far as is reasonably possible.

---

sensus fidelium appeared in texts on theological sources, but the concept was not employed commonly in theology. The authoritative source usually cited is that of Melchior Cano's (d. 1560) *De Locis Theologicis*. Cano lists four criteria to establish whether a doctrine or practice belonged to apostolic tradition of the Church, including the "present common consent of the faithful" as one of the four criteria. In other words, if there was a broad consensus and reception of a new doctrine within the life of the Church, then that would reflect the *sensus fidei/fidelium*. Cano suggested that central issues such as apostolic succession, the canon of Scripture, and the acceptance of the Roman See reflect this broad consensus.

Renowned Dominican scholar Yves Congar claims that since the early eighteenth century, the teaching authority of the Church claimed a monopoly of truth that progressively undermined the notion of the *sensus fidei/fidelium*, and Vatican II's definition of the Church as "The People of God" has initiated a corrective to this virtual marginalization of the "faithful." Another significant name is that of Cardinal John Henry Newman, who spoke of a wisdom deep in the bosom of the mystical body of Christ challenging the Church to become a "community of phronesis (practical wisdom)." The emphasis shifts to the whole church as a discerning body. The Vatican's International Theological Commission issued a document in July 2014, "*Sensus Fidei* in the Life of the Church," exploring aspects of the concept and how bishops might apply it in certain circumstances.

- *Better group relationships.* By collaborating rather than competing, group members are able to build closer relationships through the process. Resentment, rivalry, and division are minimized.
- *Better implementation of decisions.* When widespread agreement is achieved and everyone has participated in the process, strong levels of cooperation usually take place in the actions that follow. There are less likely to be disgruntled losers who might undermine or passively sabotage effective implementation of the decision.

The big challenge for most people here is the need for all views to be listened to with equal attention. For many people, listening is not a well-developed skill in comparison with the emphasis placed on talking things through.

Consensus means overwhelming agreement, and an important element is that consensus be the product of a good-faith effort to meet the interests of all stakeholders. The key indicator that a consensus has been reached is that everyone agrees they can live with the final proposal—that is, after every effort has been made to meet any outstanding interests. Thus, consensus requires that someone frame a proposal after listening carefully to everyone's interests. *Interests, by the way, are not the same as positions or demands.* Demands and positions are what people say they must have, but interests are the underlying needs or reasons that explain why people take the positions that they do.

Most consensus-building efforts set out to achieve unanimity. Along the way, however, it often becomes clear that there are holdouts—people who believe that their interests will be better served by remaining outside the emerging agreement. Should the rest of the group throw in the towel? No, this would invite blackmail (i.e., outrageous demands that have nothing to do with the issues under discussion). Most dispute-resolution professionals believe that groups or assemblies should seek unanimity but settle for overwhelming agreement that goes as far as possible toward meeting the interests of all stakeholders. It is absolutely crucial that this definition of success be clear at the outset.

Despite several attempts throughout the twentieth century to cultivate a consensual culture—in the workplace and in academia—the strategy of adversarial debate is still the favored option in the socioeconomic and political spheres. Education, legal process, and even sports endorse and adopt the same approach, frequently resulting in embittered conflicts with several losers and few winners. In the social and political domains, the heavy hand of a violent minority results in a disillusioned and disenchanted majority, many of whom feel they cannot be heard without resorting to violence. The worldwide menace of drug abuse is one glaring example.

The right to vote is an eagerly sought privilege in every culture, and today is enjoyed by most people in our world, yet the notion of empowering citizenship is virtually unknown on Planet Earth. We elect new governments on the basis of promises that are made but often suspended, denied, and discarded once the party reaches power. Faced with this dilemma, the citizens who took such pride in being able to cast a vote now realize that they are totally helpless, with no way of challenging the political corruption. Throughout the world, our leading political systems are deeply flawed and create serious regression in terms of people coming-of-age.

The art of consensus making is imperative, not merely to bring about a more peaceful and harmonious world order but also to ensure ecojustice to all creatures with whom we share Planet Earth. The evolutionary thrust of our time signals that all will grow together in a more proactive, holistic way, or all will be condemned to a dire outcome. If it comes to that, humanity itself will be the great loser. Our coming-of-age is the cusp around which so much vacillates—for our own future and that of all organic life.

After the Guru Has Disappeared

Popular religion today has been co-opted by the politics and economics of our age, thus creating a subtle but pervasive codependency, further enhanced by salacious advertising. We are continuously drawn into a highly addictive lure, a petrified raw hunger, that leaves us restless and forever seeking a redemptive panacea. People engage this dilemma in a range of different ways, some investing in hard work to make as much money as possible, others pursuing power and control. Some seek salvation through multimedia connections, others through a range of popular therapies, and still others through fundamentalist religion. All are seeking an illusionary certainty that holds them in its lure. Coming-of-age rarely happens for such people. In fact, the prospect of growing older is the very thing many of them dread.

Every age has known its liminal pushers, those who seek out alternative ways of being beyond the addictive lure of the age. In former times, it might be withdrawal to a monastery, or a life dedicated to generous and altruistic service. In our time, the call seems to be to the expansive horizons of a world growing ever more precarious in ecological terms, yet ever more promising in its cosmological and spiritual horizons. Our inherited metanarrative, rooted in patriarchal politics, economics, and religiosity, is proving ever more alienating and disempowering. It is too narrow and functional for the evolutionary aspirations of our age. How to flow within this evolutionary coming-of-age is the supreme challenge of this time, and few gurus are around to lead the way.

In the old Buddhist adage, the way is made by walking it. We lead together, in lateral collaboration, and not in linear sequence. The blueprints, if any, will be given to us from the created world; the emerging science of *biomimicry* offers some fruitful and promising examples (more in O'Murchu 2017, 72–74). The guru is no longer an imperial male, representing either the church or the academy, less so a robust individual person. The pioneering wisdom has morphed into a collective entity, *a communal process*, with networking likely to be the more generic modality (cf. Hawken 2007). Evolutionary wisdom will prove to be our more reliable resource; let's explore its promising hope.

3

Evolutionary Momentum in the Twenty-First Century

Theology must begin with evolution if it is to talk of a living God.

—Ilia Delio

We really should talk about co-evolution, rather than evolution, to remind ourselves that no species can or does evolve by itself, but that all must cooperate by adapting to the others' steps in the dance of life—by seeking their mutual consistency with one another and with the rest of their surround.

—Elizabet Sahtouris

René Descartes's declaration "I think, therefore I am" marked a new threshold in human rationality. The historical epoch is often named "the Enlightenment," otherwise called the "Age of Reason."[1]

---

[1] French historians traditionally place the Enlightenment between 1715 (the year that Louis XIV died) and 1789 (the beginning of the French Revolution). Some recent historians begin the period in the 1620s, with the start of the scientific revolution.

The powers and uses of reason had first been explored by the philosophers of ancient Greece (e.g., Plato, Aristotle), and later popularized by the philosopher Boethius (d. 526 CE) who described a human being as an individual substance subsisting of a rational nature. The Romans adopted and preserved much of Greek culture, notably including the ideas of a rational natural order and natural law. Amid the turmoil of empire, however, a new concern arose for personal salvation, and the way was paved for the triumph of the Christian religion. Christian thinkers gradually found uses for their Greco-Roman heritage. The system of thought known as Scholasticism, culminating in the work of St. Thomas Aquinas in the Middle Ages, resurrected reason as a tool of understanding but subordinated it to spiritual revelation and the revealed truths of Christianity.

By the Middle Ages, the intellectual and political edifice of Christianity became something of an impregnable fortress. In time its influence was undermined by humanism, the Renaissance, and the Protestant Reformation. The Enlightenment included a range of ideas centered on reason as the primary source of authority and legitimacy, and came to advance ideals such as liberty, progress, constitutional government, and the separation of church and state.

The Enlightenment and its modern cultural impact were widely considered as the human species' coming-of-age. The literati and intellectuals of the time, invoking the power of reason, felt that humans could take over and rule the world according to the will of a supremely rational God, who was largely a projected fantasy of imperialism come of age.[2]

As with all such historical developments, a counterculture was waiting in the wings. In the second half of the twentieth century, it began to explode, causing inevitable social and cultural

---

[2] The Jungian analyst and psychotherapist Jerome S. Bernstein has developed an anti-imperial notion of living in the borderland, not a direct opposition to rational discourse but rather an attempt to address those psychotic or pathological behaviors that characterize excessive rationalism (more in Bernstein 2006).

dislocation. Personally, I consider quantum physics to be one of the most momentous shifts into a new post-Enlightenment consciousness (more in Levy 2018). This was followed by a rapid awakening of evolutionary vision with emphasis on emergence, complexity, and growth—movements not readily subjugated to human patriarchal control.

These two features—*quantum physics* and *evolutionary science*—mark the new coming-of-age in the twenty-first century that forms the basis of this book. From these two foundational movements, I move on to outline a contemporary understanding of archetypal wisdom, which—in part 2—I suggest is the foundation stone of a great deal of the Christian gospel, with substantial implications for the new adult awakening surfacing in the twenty-first century.

Quantum Physics: The Relational Paradigm

The discovery of quantum theory in the opening decades of the twentieth century marked a momentous evolutionary shift. The rationality, quantification, and predictability that had prevailed for at least the previous five thousand years, and had been scientifically sanctioned in sixteenth-century Newtonian mechanical synthesis, now gave way to a new scientific emergence, the fuller implications of which are still under investigation and remain hugely controversial in scientific research. Cultural historian Richard Tarnas (1991) captures the shifting sands in this quote: "By the end of the third decade of the twentieth century, virtually every major postulate of the earlier scientific conception had been controverted: the atoms as solid, indestructible, and separate building blocks of nature, space and time as independent absolutes, the strict causality of all phenomena, the possibility of objective observation of nature" (356).

❄

Personal Reflection

In Ireland in the 1970s, science did not feature in my secondary education. Around age thirty, on the recommendation of a work colleague, I read my first science book ever, The Tao of Physics *by Fritjof Capra. Although several scientists have dismissed the work as New-Age nonsense, it opened me up to ways of viewing reality, with ramifications that last until the present time. Gradually I began to realize that our educational approaches to how science is taught in schools and universities militate seriously against the sense of wonder and awe science evoked in me.*

Because I came to understand and appreciate science from a philosophical and spiritual perspective, I realized ever more clearly the extensive damage done in every field of learning because of the prevalence of dualistic splitting, particularly the binary opposition of science versus religion. Instead of emphasizing the mutual enrichment of a "both-and" approach, the rational mind-set of our world continues the artificial split that violates the deep meaning of each field of wisdom, issuing in a kind of cultural depravity that inhibits millions from attaining the more mature coming-of-age explored in this book.

I continue to marvel at the explosive mystical wisdom embedded in quantum physics. It has changed my outlook in several significant ways, urging me particularly to pursue relational connections in the face of the several fragmentary dichotomies that both science and religion still uphold. I want to encourage every reader of this book to embrace the worldview of quantum physics and not be inhibited by a sense of scientific inferiority. For the noninitiated, starting out, like myself, with a minimal knowledge of science, I highly recommend Miriam Therese Winter's book Paradoxology: Spirituality in a Quantum Universe *(2009) and Paul Levy's* The Quantum Revelation *(2018). Both inspiring reads!*

✳

So complex and original is the thinking of quantum physics that mainline science itself has scarcely begun to apprehend and integrate its alternative brand of wisdom. In fact, quantum physics' foundational tenets are quite simple but earth-shattering in their consequences:

- Everything in creation is energy. It is all that is—and everything that is.
- Empty space is full of creative energy. The perceived emptiness is actually a fullness.
- The truth of reality as energy is in the very small—the subatomic realm, which is beyond ordinary human comprehension.
- In human (scientific) terms we describe energy as a wavelike process, which when humanly observed becomes a particle.
- Energy waves operate in probabilistic terms. Below the quantum level (about 10^{-9} meters), nothing can be definitely predicted (the uncertainty principle).
- Energy seems to have a preferred sense of direction— toward greater complexity and creativity.
- Energy operates according to interdependent principles, and does so on a universal process known as entanglement.
- In classical physics, if we roll a ball up a hill, we know it will not be able to roll over the hill without sufficient velocity; it will roll back down again. However, a quantum wave-particle will actually go straight through the hill and arrive at the other side. That's known as *quantum tunneling.*

- Something bigger than cause and effect is at work in the quantum realm. There are no neutral observers, but only engaged participants (more in Levy 2018).
- At the quantum level, everything is interrelated, interconnected, and interdependent; reality seems to function optimally when we engage best with this foundational relationality.

Even quantum physicists themselves are reluctant to ask: so what energizes the energy itself? I dare to suggest that this is the ultimate question for quantum physics itself. Moreover, I suspect the only satisfactory answer is *Spirit-power*. Throughout this book I call it the *Great Spirit*, a topic on which I elaborate further in the concluding chapter.

In the quantum realm, we are dealing with a mystical, experiential perception, a visceral feeling of an energy force that permeates and informs everything in creation. As an energy form, however, it is subtle, pervasive, and infused with an inherent directionality toward meaning and purpose. Quantum physics is probably the only branch of the human sciences that illuminates this ancient understanding of energy-force (more in Schafer 2013). We can also draw on religious/philosophical precedents from the ancient Chinese notion of Chi (cf. Kim 2011) and from the Vedic concept of Prana (cf. McCaul 2007; Maehle 2012). Some scholars, such as British physicist Jude Currivan (2017), feel we have moved beyond quantum physics into the realms of information and consciousness, which engage us through a more holographic understanding of the cosmic creation.

Let's make an initial link with the Judeo-Christian story. According to the popularized version of the book of Genesis, the all-powerful creator God—the cosmic engineer—is the one who set everything in motion, and before God did so, nothing at all existed. Beginnings are always taking place, without necessarily marking a definitive newness. Many contemporary Scripture scholars would balk at the imperial tenor of this explanation. The notion of "creation-out-of-nothing" (*creatio ex nihilo*) is used to emphasize God's ontological being above and beyond all created forms. The alternative account of creation, equally based on exegetical scholarship, is that of *creatio ex profundis* (Keller 2003, 155ff.). As the name implies, creation arises out of the boundless and expanding depths of the chaos-cosmos rather than being zapped into being from nothing. According to Catherine Keller, the beginning does not mark a single absolute origin but a "beginning-in-process" that is both "unoriginated and endless."

Infinite creative possibilities open out from the formlessness, undifferentiated, and bottomless abyss of primordial chaos (including the controversial notion of the multiverse). There is great depth and darkness to life, and it is a fertile darkness, or what quantum physics names as the *creative vacuum* (see Davidson 2004). The darksome deep is an ambivalent origin, in contrast to a creation under the mechanism of control and mastery that *ex nihilo* offers. In the beginning is formless, primal chaos, evoking a feminine, tehomic language and a refutation of divine omnipotence.

The Evolutionary Imperative

A quantum universe knows neither beginning nor end, categories important to humans who carry the patriarchal urge to dominate and control. Creation is a process, not a product, a complex trajectory forever reworking its past, but for the greater part guided by the lure of the open-ended future. Creation is neither random nor predetermined. A quantum universe seems to "know" what it is about—the intelligent creation Fred Hoyle described many years ago. Our major problem seems to be that we humans have not yet evolved the humility and transparency to surrender ourselves to this cosmic evolutionary imperative.

Before proceeding, we need to note the conventional use of the term "evolution," allegedly inspired by the great Charles Darwin (1809–1882).[3] Evolution describes the impact of *change* in the

---

[3] Scholars writing from a more religious perspective claim that the

inherited characteristics of biological populations over successive generations. This process results in *greater diversity* at every level of biological organization, including species, individual organisms, and molecules such as DNA and proteins. Existing patterns of biodiversity have been shaped both by speciation and by *extinction*. Darwin (c. 1859) was the first to formulate a scientific argument for the theory of evolution by means of natural selection. The selection itself was based on the natural variety of creatures, some of which were fitter than others (hence the notion of the *survival of the fittest*). The geneticist Gregory Mendel (d. 1884) contributes the additional factor of genetic mutations; although genes are inherited in a predictable fashion, changes in genes can occur randomly, and they arise from environmental influences, all contributing to the notion of *novelty* in evolutionary developments.

In the twentieth century, the priest-paleontologist Pierre Teilhard de Chardin (d. 1959) popularized a religious understanding of evolution. In fact, Teilhard's religious perspective was largely linked to the ideological superiority of the Christian religion, as understood at that time. However, his new synthesis was sufficiently robust to launch further breakthroughs, limited in scientific terms, but potentially explosive for both spirituality and theology.

An American Franciscan Sister, Ilia Delio, a theologian at Villanova University, is now emerging as the single finest exponent of Teilhard's vision and its relevance for science and cosmology in the twenty-first century. She defines evolution in these words (2013):

> Evolution is less a mechanism than a process—a constellation of law, chance, spontaneity, and deep time. . . .
> Evolution is not simply a biological mechanism of gene swapping or environmental pressure. It is the unfolding and development of consciousness in which conscious-

---

atheistic tenor of contemporary Darwinian evolution belongs more to the neo-Darwinians rather than to Darwin himself, as argued by theologian Elizabeth Johnson (2014).

ness plays a significant role in the process of convergence and complexification. Evolution gives rise to religion when consciousness unfolds in a "thou-embraced-I." (xvi, 98)

The evolutionary imperative that I describe is not a cultural phenomenon that we can take or leave. Nor is it a movement over which we have human control. To the contrary, it is no longer a case of us evolving within a process over which we have a measure of human control. Rather the truth is that *we are being evolved*, in a momentous trust within which we allow ourselves to become an integral part, or otherwise we become increasingly alienated from life. I am not in any way suggesting that all is determined, and that we have no choice other than to get involved. Our coming-of-age is a wake-up call to realize that we are a derived species, creatures of a cosmic-planetary evolutionary process in which the growth and progress of each entity—ourselves included—is only possible when we opt to integrate our becoming with that larger reality.

Evolution has now entered even religious discourse, and evolution denotes change, fluidity, and flexibility. Contrary to earlier epochs, and particularly those of the Age of Reason, the coming-of-age in our time invites us to enlarged, more complex horizons. Many resist these quantum leaps, and their negative reactions receive considerable media attention. Those who flow with the process, *allowing ourselves to become more evolved*, and befriend it proactively receive less favorable attention and are often ostracized as postmodernists, anarchists, or social mavericks. In the hope of bringing clarity and coherence into this complex and rapidly evolving landscape, I delineate the following key features of our evolutionary consciousness today. These may also be considered some of the key elements in the coming-of-age explored throughout this book.

Sense of direction. For the neo-Darwinians, evolution is a random force without a predictable sense of direction. It resembles a blind battle of wits in which the strong win and the weak lose. The renowned Stephen J. Gould endorsed this view, but toward the end of his life conceded that while he could not entertain the notion of purpose in evolution, he would accept that it had a preferred sense of direction. For me, three words captivate this preference: *growth-change-complexity*. We see this tripartite development at several levels of daily life:

- Everything within and around us *grows*; that seems an indisputable fact of the natural and human worlds.
- We perceive *change* all around us, and this involves decline and death. Such disintegration is not an evil, nor is it the consequence of sin (see Rom. 6:23), but a God-given dimension of all creation.
- At every level of life, evolution seems to move toward greater sophistication and *complexity*, a process always inclusive of the death and disintegration already noted.

Another aspect of directionality is the shift from the inherited claim that evolution happens by repeating the successful patterns of the past; in other words, everything is driven from behind. Formal religions also adopt this view. Theologian John F. Haught almost single-handedly challenges this view, asserting that it is the lure of the future more than anything else that informs the evolutionary imperative. Here, I am adopting a key insight of philosopher Karl Popper, articulated anew by Haught (2010; 2015), that the direction of evolution takes shape primarily in response to the *lure of the future*, and not merely solidifying what has served us well in the past. In the words of John Haught (2015), "Evolution, viewed theologically, means that creation is still happening and that God is creating and saving the world not *a retro*, that is, by pushing it forward out of the past, but *ab ante*, by calling it from up ahead" (52). Theologically, I understand that the central attraction of the lure of the future is a fruit and wisdom of the Holy Spirit.

Here we encounter perhaps one of the more controversial dimensions of the coming-of-age I am exploring, namely, the adoption of a multidisciplinary interface. In the academic world, religion and science, for the greater part, are still dualistically opposed, but not in the emerging spiritual landscape of our time. And this leads me to consider a second significant feature of the evolutionary imperative.

Driven by consciousness. Back in 1931 the renowned physicist Max Planck observed that consciousness is the fundamental stuff of all creation, and that matter is derived therefrom. In this context, consciousness denotes information as a driving energetic force (see Currivan 2017, 2–20). It is not merely an endowment of human intelligence but an empowering quality of creation in all its aspects and at every stage of its long historical evolution. Aliveness, therefore, can no longer be reserved to human beings. On the contrary, we know that everything that constitutes our embodiment as earthlings is given to us from earth itself, as a living organism, itself energized from the larger cosmic web of life.

But from where does the cosmic creation obtain this resourcefulness? Once more we are called to transcend inherited academic distinctions and transgress the rationality that has been so foundational to our inherited information. We move to a higher level of discourse, in pursuit of a deeper integration. In theological terms, it is the Holy Spirit that enlivens all that exists (cf. Boff 2015; Haughey 2015), an attribution I amplify further in the final chapter of this book in terms of the contribution to the Great Spirit. How does our coming-of-age, as a species and as people of faith, embrace and integrate this larger sense of aliveness? And what are the implications for Christian faith and practice in the twenty-first century? These questions engage us throughout the book.

The all-embracing sense of aliveness unfolds along an evolutionary trajectory that transcends simple cause-and-effect, with a sense of direction that is open and unpredictable, always evolving into greater complexity (for further elaboration, see Delio 2015; Stewart 2000). The culture of patriarchal certainty, and hierarchical ordering (as evidenced in several religious doctrines), is increasingly understood as an anthropocentric projection that alienates humans by separating us from the womb of our becoming and attributing to us an elevated status increasingly viewed as exploitative and dangerous. We have ended up with a perverted anthropology that has seriously distorted how we perceive and understand several elements of faith, including our Christian understanding of incarnation.

Imbued with paradox. By postulating a consciousness-driven creation, probably fueled by a Spirit-infused creative energy, we are reframing rather than denying the chanciness that the neo-Darwinians claim is inherent to creation at large. Without this chanciness there is in fact no room for creativity or freedom. Certain levels of negative fallout are inevitable, but in the context of consciousness they take on a much more complex yet coherent meaning, central to which is the notion of *paradox*.

Creation's evolutionary unfolding is endowed with the paradoxical interplay of creation-cum-destruction, an unceasing cyclic rhythm of birth-death-rebirth. Major religions tend to dismiss this paradox as a fundamental flaw requiring divine salvific intervention, particularly through the death and resurrection of the historical Jesus. This enduring paradox is central to the entire fabric of universal life. It includes those puzzling and at times frightening features like pain, suffering, calamity, earthquakes, breakdown, decline, and death. These are not evils to be eliminated; they are foundational to all growth, change, and complexity throughout creation.

A useful example is that of earthquakes. In scientific terms an earthquake is a shifting in the earth's tectonic plates, which among other things involves a clearing away of excess wastage, thus facilitating the earth-body to function in a healthier way. If we had no earthquakes, we would not have the viable planet we have today, with its vast array of life-forms and living systems. Earthquakes are essential—absolutely crucial—to the viability of Planet Earth.

The religious believer will ask: Is this how God created the world? Did the same God also create the paradoxes that characterize our creation? The religionist wants to hear a negative response, but that would be inauthentic. The creative life force—divine or otherwise—is also the source and sustenance of the destruction. Through and through—at every level from that of the macroscopic universe to the microscopic bacterium—the same evolutionary process is observable: creation is endowed with the paradox of creation and destruction, otherwise named as a process of birth-death-rebirth. It cannot be otherwise. The paradox is the foundation for freedom and creativity. Get rid of the paradox and all we have left is total nihilism.

Central to these reflections is the place that death plays in the grand scheme of things. Every major religion views death as an evil to overcome and eliminate. The coming-of-age discerned throughout this book very much involves embracing and befriending death as an essential feature of all growth and development. It is the human denunciation of death and our addictive drives to get rid of it that cause enormous amounts of meaningless death throughout the world today.

Beyond dualistic splitting. The dominant metaphysical worldview of our time, developed in classical Greek times, also favored the philosophy of divide and conquer, thus segmenting wisdom and knowledge into binary opposites (dualisms) and uniform categories, alien to the multidisciplinary and transdisciplinary philosophy of our age. According to this newer philosophy, a multidisciplinary perspective is necessary in order to comprehend the complex, mysterious nature of all living reality. Consequently, Scripture scholars in particular are increasingly adopting a multidisciplinary orientation in their research and discernment, embracing a range of social sciences and the wisdom of ancient history, combined with the corroborative evidence of archaeological discoveries; for the theological implications, see Kelly (2015). Contrary to the fear expressed by fundamentalists, such a broad interdisciplinary base, with its new quality of consciousness, does not diminish the truth of faith, but for a growing body of adult faith-seekers enriches and deepens their spirituality.

Lateral thinking. Much of Christian theology and its ensuing spirituality are defined and described in terms of classical Greek metaphysics, rational thought, and logical argument. It is a linear, sequential process favored by dominant males seeking control and mastery through rational discourse. It is a strategy alien to evolutionary unfolding, lacking in the creativity, imagination, and intuition necessary if we are to apprehend the complexities of this age and every other. Beyond the traditional affiliation with Scholastic philosophy, theology must now embrace a multidisciplinary dynamic to engage the lateral consciousness of the twenty-first century and the coming-of-age that is required if we are to engage the new emergencies of our time.

Spirituality. All over the contemporary world, mainline religion is in recession (with the possible exception of Islam), yielding pride of place either to more amorphous spiritual offshoots or to violent ideologies that will eventually destroy the very religion they seek to safeguard and promote. Nearly all formal religious traditions embody imperial sentiment, a derogatory view of creation, and a distinctly male, patriarchal bias. An alternative spiritual hunger has surfaced (and has been suppressed) many times in the history of the great religions; it sometimes morphs into a phenomenon known as mysticism, which enjoys a distinctive revival in recent decades (see Johnson and Ord 2012). Spirituality marks an enlarged horizon of religious sentiment, with several strong resonances with the unfolding biblical wisdom of our time.

Cooperation. Evolution is not solely dependent on the survival of the fittest but rather on the triumph of cooperation. For John Stewart (2000) cooperation is evolution's arrow: "Cooperators will inherit the earth, and eventually the universe" (8). However, it has to be a quality of cooperation that can embrace and integrate legitimate self-interest. This is the kind of integration that wise elders desire. And it is remarkably similar to the supreme goal of both Judaism and Christianity: love God! And to do that, one has to love the neighbor, which is genuinely possible only when we learn to love ourselves (cf. Lev. 19:18; Mk. 12:29–30). Genuine self-interest is not contrary to faith in God nor to faith in evolution; it is the prerequisite for both.

Discernment. Christian discernment describes the human effort to discover, appropriate, and integrate God's desires for our growth and development as people of faith. In its popular (Ignatian) sense, it is very much an individual process between the person and God, with the spiritual director acting as a guide or facilitator. Group discernment is a more loosely defined process often invoked at religious gatherings and in areas of pastoral accountability (more in Liebert 2015).

In the ecclesiastical context, discernment is understood to be the divinely bestowed prerogative of the teaching authority of the church, to which all other forms of discernment must be accountable. In a world and church becoming increasingly suspicious of the integrity and truth of institutional guidance, the task of discernment for the future will become much more localized, dialogically mediated, and informed by the skills and wisdom of systems theory (in other words, multidisciplinary). Increasingly, personal and group discernment will interweave, with wisdom from the ground up commanding much stronger credibility than that which comes from the top down. Theological and scriptural insight will no longer be seen as a reserve of the academic scholar but rather a dialogical process, reclaiming and reviving the often-neglected notion of the *sensus fidelium.*

These evolutionary propensities mark a seismic shift from a worldview in which we were "captivated by the spell of solidity, the fallacy of fixity, the illusion of immobility, the semblance of stasis," as described by Phipps (2012), who goes on to say, "but the evolution revolution is starting to break that spell. We are realizing that we are, in fact, not standing on solid ground. But neither are we adrift in a meaningless universe. . . . We are part and parcel of a vast process of becoming" (26). He also identifies three characteristics (Phipps 2012, 32) common to evolutionary thinkers (and to the wise elders) of the twenty-first century:

- Evolutionaries are cross-disciplinary generalists.
- They develop the capacity to cognize the vast timescales of our evolutionary history.
- They embody a new spirit of optimism.

And this spirit of optimism is one important dimension in the spiritual coming-of-age being explored in the present work. Our interconnected, information-saturated world yearns for a new unifying synthesis that will empower us to transcend so many divisive ideologies we have inherited from the past. Despite ethnic tribalism and the political bantering to defend national identities, the coming together of the human species as one entity—celebrating what we share in common, rather than nursing rancor over what divides us—is a central feature of the evolutionary imperative of this age.

To the politicians, the economists, the religionists—those who cling to patriarchal domination—it sounds bizarrely idealistic and optimistic. So does every utopian dream, but without such dreams our species is unlikely to survive the current onslaught of voracious globalization, economic exploitation, tribal violence, and ecological devastation. Ours is an age in crisis, birthing an alternative strategy not merely for survival but for flourishing, because that is the deep hunger that has characterized our species from time immemorial. It touches psychic depths that rationality and patriarchal logic can never comprehend, as indicated vividly by Jungian analyst Jerome Bernstein (2006). It evokes another dynamic—a very different coming-of-age—described by mystics and sages as the power of the archetype.

The Archetypal Viewpoint

Some readers of this book may not be acquainted with the notion of *archetypes*, but unfortunately, many are likely to have been exposed to a negative appraisal. Derived from two Greek words—*arche* meaning first and *tupos* meaning type or form—archetypes emerge from what Carl G. Jung called the *collective unconscious,* an envelope of creative energy from which everything in creation is begotten. The five primordial archetypes are Ether, Air, Fire, Water, and Earth. These foundational energies, either singularly or in combination, give rise to all other archetypes.

Everything in the natural world is endowed with the energy of archetypes, including plants and human beings. For Keiron Le Grice (2010), "Archetypes might thus be seen as the predominantly interior experience of the cosmological powers—as the universe's natural dynamics experienced intrapsychically" (251). Building on the earlier research of Richard Tarnas (2006), Le Grice provides a fine overview of how astrology can illuminate the numinous and enduring power of certain energy patterns detectable throughout the universe, which affect our human lives to a degree that as yet is poorly understood. In scientific terms, the research of physicist Brian Swimme (see Swimme and Tucker 2011), on what he describes as the cosmological powers,[4] provides a more solid ground for a range of ideas that feel speculative and far-fetched to many contemporary people. Throughout this book I argue that the personal integration of such cosmological interconnectedness is a central feature of the coming-of-age explored in these pages.

All human aspiration, desire, and action arise from the energetic creativity of archetypes that dwell in the collective unconscious of universal life. Archetypes have been adopted by both

---

[4] The Christian reader may be aware of the pioneering work of biblical scholar and peace activist Walter Wink (1992), who wrote a series of books on "the powers" to describe transhuman cultural forces that inhibit or undermine particularly our human attempts at nonviolent justice for person and planet alike. To the best of my knowledge, Wink does not employ wisdom related to archetypes to make sense of these "powers." One wonders if his insights might not be related to the negative impact of archetypal energy, when the emerging wisdom gets locked into, or blocked by, the Jungian notion of the complexes. For Hillman (1975), "soul" is the bridge that realigns the distortions that arise when archetypal aspirations are reduced to the needs of the heroic ego.

anthropology and psychology, and more recently in cosmology-based studies, to name and explain those sublime energetic forces that transcend our rational and commonsense modes of understanding. All archetypal truth is spiritual in nature, often transcending the doctrines and structures of the formal religions and forever luring us into a deeper search for meaning. Jungian theorist James Hillman claims that archetypal psychology is theophonic, describing the inmost soul—not necessarily the deities of formal religions—that grounds everything in deep meaning (more in Hillman 1975; 1983).

I leave it to the reader to delve into the intricacies of Jung's notion of the archetypes, upon which a vast literature exists (see the fine overview in Stevens 2002). For the present work, the following summary captivates the key ingredients:

> The archetypes were conceived by Jung as principles that are both instinctual and spiritual, both natural and transcendent. Indeed, such is the complex character of the archetypes that Jung felt it necessary to employ a wide variety of terms to describe them: gods, patterns of behavior, conditioning factors, primordial images, unconscious dominants, organizing forms, formative principles, instinctual powers, dynamisms—to give but a few examples. He suggests, furthermore, that the archetypes are "active, living dispositions, ideas in the Platonic sense that perform and continually influence our thoughts, feelings, and actions." Jung therefore situates his theory of archetypes firmly in the mythic-Platonic tradition. Like the mythological gods, the archetypes are the formative principles, superordinate to human consciousness and will, that structure, order, and animate our life experience. (Le Grice 2010, 158)

Additionally, theologian Paul F. Knitter (1985) describes archetypes as predispositions towards the formation of images, a-priori powers of representation, inbuilt stirrings or lures that, if we can feel and follow them, will lead us into the depths of what we are and where we are going. They might be called messages-in-code, which we must decode and bring to our conscious awareness. It is difficult to speak about what these messages contain. Their general contents, Jung tells us, have to do with light and darkness, death and rebirth, wholeness, sacrifice, and redemption. He saw such archetypes as the common seedbed of all religions. (57)

Finally, for the purposes of the present work, a description from William Bausch (1984) is worth citing:

That is why certain basic myths called archetypal keep popping up. Some are the sharing of food, denoting the sharing of the very substance that keeps one alive; hence the supreme hospitality, brotherhood, fellowship; the shedding of blood as a loss of vitality, and drinking it as drinking the source of life. There are Gods who died and rose again to explain the seasons. Miracles were used as proof of divine power. Virgin births were spoken of. The point is that these symbols are not unique to Christianity nor should they be. They are basic myths that explain humanity's eternal hopes, answers to the meaning of life, birth, death, tragedy and suffering. (70–71)

Following are some of the key ingredients of archetypal wisdom. Parallels with quantum physics are immediately obvious:

• *The archetype has no form of its own, but it acts as an "organizing principle" on the things we see or do.* It works the way that instincts work in Freud's theory. Everybody recognizes the power of instinct and its rootedness in biological behavior. The corresponding psychic forces are the archetypes. They are equally real—in fact, more really real—but not accessible merely through rational thought or biological behavior. As a simple example, human sexuality is an archetypal lure for deep intimate bonding while secondarily being an instinct for human reproduction. The archetype provides the larger and deeper sphere of meaning.

Rational logic in itself rarely opens us up to archetypal meaning. Imagination, intuition, and discerning wisdom are far more reliable resources, even in a borderland (pathological) context (cf. Bernstein 2006). Leonard Shlain, author of the bestselling *Art and Physics* (Shlain 1991), proposes that the process of learning alphabetic literacy rewired the human brain, with profound consequences for culture and the future direction of evolution. Making remarkable connections across a wide range of subjects including brain function, anthropology, history, and religion, Shlain argues that literacy reinforced the brain's linear, abstract, predominantly masculine left hemisphere at the expense of the holistic, iconic, feminine right one. This shift upset the balance between men and women, initiating the disappearance of goddesses, the abhorrence of images, and, in literacy's early stages, the decline of women's political status. Patriarchy and misogyny followed.

The archetypal tends to be rooted in lived experience that transcends the age of civilization (approximately the past five thousand years) in favor of older evolutionary wisdom, dealing with what today some call deep time. For instance, if the Christian notion of incarnation celebrates God's solidarity with human life, why do we locate it in the historical context of the past few thousand years? Why not locate it when God's creativity first became manifest in our human species some 7 million years ago? And if incarnation carries archetypal significance for embodiment, why restrict the process to human bodies? Why can't incarnation be the celebration of all embodied reality from cosmos to bacteria? (See more in O'Murchu 2017.)

• *In the archetypal realm time signifies a great deal more than the scientific notion of space-time.* Beyond our felt need for rational, linear measurement, we are asked to embrace the mystical notion of the eternal now. Here, past, present, and future coalesce into a new sense of continuity often echoed in John's Gospel and recurring in the mystical literature of all the great religions.

Particularly significant is the anthropological context, viewed in archetypal terms. As a species we have evolved within an evolutionary story of some *7 million* years (more in O'Murchu 2008), an ancient sacred narrative that has been reduced and squeezed into the anthropocentric bottleneck of the age of civilization (approximately the past five thousand years). This shriveled anthropology has produced a number of cultural distortions, including central features of all the major religions. Ever since early Christian times, we have assessed the humanity of Jesus in terms of the robust, separate, rational individual of Aristotelian philosophy (often described today as the buffered self). Jesus, however, contextualized his life and mission within the realm of the kingdom of God, portraying a very different anthropology, with the relational horizon radically to the fore (more in chapter 6).

• *Is the archetypal another name—a secular one—for the divine? No!* The archetype helps to illuminate the divine empowerment emanating from the collective unconscious. In ancient "pagan" religions, certain gods and goddesses were given archetypal significance; for example, many different pantheons have a Mother Goddess and a Father God, a god or goddess of death, and a sky god or goddess. Earlier I referred to Ether, Air, Fire, Water, and Earth as the five primordial archetypes. Science and rational wisdom can describe the materiality of any of those elements, but in the long history of humanity each has had several symbolic meanings as well; this latter significance arises from our propensity to perceive archetypally, to respond to the lure of the Great Spirit mediated through the collective unconscious.

John C. Robinson (2016) offers a prehistoric context in which he claims that our earliest ancestors sensed consciousness as mysterious, alive, omnipresent, and holy, a sentience that created the perception of living in a divine landscape of sacred beings. With the development of language, we learned to name and explain everything, creating a secondary world of thought. As conceptualization overlaid pantheistic consciousness, humankind's capacity for direct experience of the sacred diminished, generating a deep and poignant longing for a savior to restore the divine world. These archetypal figures reflect a common longing for a new Divine Human. Rather than being copycat myths, they represent allegories of humanity's universal mystical potential for divine incarnation and the restoration of a sacred universe. The Divine Human comes to heal the culture's abandonment of the realized divine.

Personal Reflection

*We have now reached a threshold in the argument of this book that requires a moment to pause, attempting to ground the grand theories in human experience and make clearer what is entailed in the coming-of-age I allude to throughout this book. Teilhard de Chardin's writings played a significant role in my own coming-of-age. While struggling to make sense of Scholastic philosophy, in my early twenties, quite by chance I discovered Teilhard and devoured his books—*Hymn of the Universe *and* The Divine Milieu *being the first I read. Teilhard's evolutionary wisdom touched the recesses of my being and rejuvenated my faith beyond my wildest expectations. In an assigned seminary essay I cited Teilhard at length, earning myself a heavy reprimand that I was dabbling in dangerous and misleading pseudospirituality that no responsible clerical student should be accessing. I guess I was at a life stage where I relished forbidden fruit; the reprimand reinforced rather than diminished my evolutionary enthusiasm.*

At that time in my life, Teilhard's grand evolutionary optic did not evoke a cosmological or planetary awakening (that would come some twenty years later), but instead opened doors into anthropology and paleontology (the study of human origins). My understanding of incarnation took something of a quantum leap. Why confine God's embrace of our human reality to a narrow time span of two thousand years? Surely the incarnating God was already fully at work those many thousands of years ago, when our species first evolved from the African soil! Not until 2008 did I pluck up the courage to come out and declare in writing my expanded new incarnational horizon (cf. O'Murchu 2008).

Meanwhile, the evolutionary seeds sown in my heart had been sprouting in two divergent but connected directions. My studies in psychology in the early 1980s introduced me to the esoteric vision of the renowned psychologist Carl G. Jung. Although not encouraged in the academic circles of my formalized studies, I once more was attracted to the forbidden fruit and especially Jung's notion of archetypes and the collective unconscious. As I recall, this is where I first encountered the counterintuitive insights of quantum physics, and with minimal scientific training ventured on to pen what was to become the masterpiece of my writing career, Quantum Theology, *first published in 1997.*

Over several years, a synthesis has been taking shape, a psychic and intellectual maturation, which in the present book I am seeking to articulate with greater clarity than on previous occasions. I trust it is my intellectual spirit coming of age in a deeper and more integrated way. The synthesis is based on three interconnected threads:

   • *Quantum physics, suggesting an understanding of the universe as energized and empowered by a spiritual life force, which Christian theology names as the Holy Spirit, and I rename as the Great Spirit. The ensuing cosmology, as outlined by a contemporary physicist, Jude Currivan (2017), transcends all the mechanistic modeling and anthropocentric desire for control that characterize classical science.*

* *Evolution, the unfolding process whereby the underlying creative energy forever seeks out new ways of interconnecting and complexifying, a process that builds on the success of the past but is governed primarily by the lure of the future (the imperative of the Great Spirit). In this evolutionary context humans are called to be servants to an unfolding wisdom over which we have no patriarchal control. Trust, not power, is the core virtue we need.*

* *Archetypal wisdom. A creation infused and sustained by the Great Spirit is embedded in a quality of intelligence that outwits all our human learning and forever lures us into a deeper mystical-type mode of understanding. Because we have been so indoctrinated with philosophical and scientific rationality, this more foundational wisdom has been subverted, ridiculed, and demonized. My sense is that we humans are unlikely to make a concerted effort at retrieving such deeper wisdom until we are propelled by some major human catastrophe.*

Embracing this threefold dynamic, in the second part of this book I revisit the Jesus story, indicating that much of this alternative wisdom is precisely what guided and sustained Jesus in that unique project that gave birth to our Christian faith.

Christianity's New Coming-of-Age

Historically and culturally, Jesus belongs to the Jewish cultural milieu. His early education and formation are very likely to have been in a conventional Jewish context, where culture and religion were essentially one and the same. While the Jewish context remains crucial for interpretation, an archetypal evaluation requires us to look beyond Jesus the Jew to one who becomes an archetypal representation of a cosmic, planetary, and transcultural way of being human.[5] In our contemporary, capitalistic-driven culture, that way of being human is largely unknown, apart from some indigenous peoples scattered around the globe.

Throughout this book, I propose that, for those of us embracing a Christian faith, Jesus fulfills an archetypal role. In Jesus is embodied a unique integration of the human as earthly, yet poised for a process of transformation that converts the merely human into a more radiant expression of being fully alive. The purpose of such archetypal modeling is not for the glorification of the beneficiary himself or herself, but for those with whom the archetypal one is interconnected. Such a personality is likely to be hugely attractive, yet at times repulsive because of the dislocation that is likely to ensue for conventional living. Think of the prophets in the Hebrew Scriptures: loved and admired, but also dreaded and frequently misunderstood.

In adopting this archetypal portrayal, I am suggesting that the inherited distinction between the humanity and divinity of Jesus is so overloaded with cultural and ideological baggage that it is

---

[5] In Küng (1974), we read, "For Christians then Jesus is certainly a teacher, but at the same time also essentially more than a teacher: he is in person the living, archetypal embodiment of his cause" (545); "Christianity can ultimately be and become relevant only by activating—as always, in theory and practice—the memory of Jesus as ultimately archetypal" (124). For a classic articulation of Jesus as an archetypal human exemplar, see the doctoral thesis of the late Walter Wink (2002), biblical scholar and advocate of nonviolent resistance, in which he writes, "Divinity is fully realized humanity. Only God is, as it were, human. The goal of life then is not to become something we are not—divine—but to become what we truly are—human. . . . Obviously, God is not just human. Nature symbols are used to speak of the nonhuman aspects of God. . . . The last thing our world needs today is another anthropocentric theology that ignores the violence being done to God's creation. . . . In place of anthropocentrism, we need anthropocosmism (human relatedness to the cosmos)" (26, 29). More on Wink's archetypal outline in chapter 5.

no longer capable of delivering the maturity that comes with age. Because we get ensnared in so many tropes related to power, domination, imperialism, and so on, we run the risk of bypassing the profound wisdom that can be so liberating and empowering. In breaking fresh ground, and thus reworking inherited wisdom, the archetypal embraces foundational depths and illuminates afresh several features of the Christian gospel that have been excessively rationalized in patriarchal rhetoric and frequently distorted by the maligning power of imperial management.

In several passages in the letters of St. Paul (especially his letter to the Romans), archetypal aspiration seems to be a central feature. What constitutes the new Adam, meant to replace the old one? Who and what is the Spirit that outwits the letter of the Law? And what is the novelty in the new covenant to which disciples of Jesus are called? Consider this passage, from 1 Corinthians 3:13–18:

> We are not like Moses, who would put a veil over his face to keep the Israelites from gazing at it while the radiance was fading away. But their minds were made dull, for to this day the same veil remains when the old covenant is read. It has not been removed, because only in Christ is it taken away. Even to this day, when Moses is read, a veil covers their hearts. But whenever anyone turns to the Lord, the veil is taken away. Now the Lord is the Spirit, and where the Spirit of the Lord is, there is freedom. And we, who with unveiled faces all reflect the Lord's glory, are being transformed into his likeness with ever-increasing glory, which comes from the Lord who is the Spirit.

According to Galatians 3:15–22, Paul uses the term law (*nomos*) to refer to the covenant at Sinai, which is focused on the giving of the Ten Commandments, the law that curses and enslaves. He contrasts this with the promise (*epangellia*) (cf. Gal. 5:14), usually understood as the gift of unconditional love. Here we detect even a new vocabulary: *promise, spirit, love, freedom.* These words are not entirely new—to either Christianity or any other world religion. The problem is that we have not internalized them in the adult coming-of-age toward which Christianity and other religions have been stretching for centuries. The time has come to take the quantum leap. Hopefully, this book offers a contribution (however small) toward that evolutionary breakthrough.

Before proceeding to part 2, in which I seek to reframe the Christian story in archetypal terms, and thus illuminate the additional coming-of-age challenging Christian believers today, I outline briefly some of the inherited baggage that first needs to be discarded. Much of this outdated and ingrained wisdom is no longer useful for the new quality of discernment that characterizes our time. More daunting still is the growing realization that we have saddled the historical Jesus with several patriarchal projections that have distorted as well as undermined his liberating and empowering message.

4

Can Christianity Survive?

Faith is not settled belief but living process. The claim of absolute truth is the greatest single obstruction to theological honesty.

—Catherine Keller

If God creates, loves, and covenants with the flesh, why do we inherit a tradition in theology that speaks so vehemently against it?

—Elizabeth Johnson

Christianity today is a world religion of some 2.2 billion people, its single biggest denomination being that of (Roman) Catholicism, comprising some 1.2 billion members. It has always been a highly diverse religion, even in its very origins (see Dunn 1977). Over time, the legacy of Constantine (272–337), and his irrational desire for control and conformity, created a monolithic overlay whereby allegiance was judged by fidelity to a fixed, unchanging set of rules and structures, thus betraying that foundational diversity, which was gradually deemed to be deviant and heretical.

The legacy of Constantine also endorsed the rationalistic anthropology of Aristotle, which, when combined with Constantine's addiction to power, left Christians with a systemic co-dependency that prevailed into the twentieth century and is still discernible in most Christian denominations. I am alluding to that parent-child sense of dependency that prevents adults from coming of age in order to appropriate their faith in a more mature adult enculturation.

Discerning Authentic Foundations

Throughout the twentieth century, Scripture scholars devoted a great deal of time and energy to researching the historical Jesus, trying to piece together what an actual historical profile would look like. Perhaps what has been most valuable in this endeavor is not what we have discovered about Jesus as a historical person (which, in truth, is relatively little), but what we have learned about the cultural context into which Jesus came and within which he lived and ministered.

Personal Reflection

I came into my adult years with one unquestionable truth: the Catholic Church is not merely the one true Church but in fact the only authentic world religion. All world religions were dismissed and denounced as pagan, and my inherited sense of other Christian denominations was one of hostility and suspicion.

My internalization of such Catholicism was based primarily on fear and the need to placate a demanding God to whom I would have to render an account at the end of my life. On the basis of that final accountability, my eternal destiny would be judged for weal or for woe.

In my early twenties the first cracks appeared, something I did not recognize until several years later. An awakening was beginning to happen; the coming-of-age would follow much later. I began to suspect that the watertight Catholic system embodied a notion of God that did not match the humanity of Jesus toward which theology was pointing me. Intuitively I was encountering a God of love rather than a God of judgment; once again, it would be several years later before I could internalize that insight.

I suspect it was my approaching mid-life stage, perhaps around my fortieth year, in which I began to let go of the Catholic monopoly. This process had two stages. The first was a deepening theological awareness of the kingdom of God as a central feature of my Christian faith, forcing me to confront the fact that my Catholicism was (and is) just one denomination of a much larger and comprehensive sense of faith. Now I had to wrestle with the fact that it was my fidelity to Jesus, in terms of the kingdom of God, that would need to take priority—not merely my allegiance to Catholicism. It became all too clear that being a good Catholic was no guarantee that I would automatically be a good Christian.

The second coming-of-age has occurred only in the past ten years. It arises from my reflections on a phrase from the Sermon on the Mount: "Seek first the Kingdom of God and its righteousness, and all these things shall be yours as well" (Matt. 6:33). These days, there is little in the Gospels that I take at face value, but this Matthean verse feels like a primordial truth. A starting point in our Christian story has been seriously compromised. Throughout several centuries we have not given first place to the kingdom of God; instead, a lot of other imperial values (and systems) have taken priority.

Striving to honor that priority ("Seek first . . .") has now become my life's work. It requires several adjustments in both beliefs and practices. Even the prevailing kingly language has to be changed and replaced (as I indicate in chapter 6). I suspect this quest for deep truth will preoccupy me for the rest of my life.

❄

One helpful way to recapture the early emergence of the Christian faith is to consider it in three time blocks, each consisting of approximately thirty-five years. We begin with the lifetime of the historical Jesus, 0–35 CE, followed by the early evolution of the Christian community between 35 and 70 CE, and finally consider the aftermath of the Great Roman War throughout the period 65–100 CE.

Scholars believe that Jesus may have been born as early as 7 BCE and was crucified sometime between 30 and 33 CE. He was born into a Jewish family and would have grown up in an environment replete with Jewish devotion and religious observance. Contemporary Scripture scholars tend to highlight his Jewish faith and assume that he would have lived out that faith as a loyal, faithful, and conventional Jew. Consequently, several conclude that it was the reform of Judaism, rather than the founding of a new religion, that was Jesus's primary concern. Some even consider Christianity to be an anti-Semitic deviation to which history has attributed an exaggerated importance.

The Jewishness of Jesus strikes me as being a very complex question, which I suspect current scholarship tends to overstate. Undoubtedly, there is a persistent anti-Semitic undercurrent—in the Gospels and throughout history—that needs to be resolved. We also need to remember that the majority of Scripture scholars are themselves the products of formal church (or religion)—often mandated by church authorities to become Scripture scholars, because of their exemplary allegiance to church-based faith—who all too easily can project on to Jesus their own understanding of religious fidelity.

Throughout the Gospels there are hints that Jesus was different. He seems to have reinterpreted—and stretched to great lengths—several aspects of his inherited religion. He seems to have been particularly critical of religious authorities of every type, and he readily transcended required observances for worship, ritual, and social boundaries. Contrary to his Jewish contemporaries for Jesus, the twin poles of holiness and sacrifice were particularly problematic. Michael Hardin (2010) suggests that, for Jesus, "holiness is not a solution but a problem. Holiness caused ostracizing and exclusion; mercy brought reconciliation and re-socializing. Holiness depended on gradation and hierarchy; mercy broke through all barriers. Holiness differentiated persons on the basis of honor, wealth, family tree, religious affiliation; mercy recognized that God honors all, loves all, and blesses all" (75).

Jesus exhibited a passionate desire for the justice and freedom proclaimed by the ancient prophets. He seemed to favor the open countryside and the marketplaces rather than the sacred domain of temple or synagogue. He loved the poor and championed their liberation through healing and social empowerment. He spoke a highly subversive message in parable stories and in sagelike wisdom. And he did not seem too concerned about the lofty apocalyptic hope in a future life promising eternal salvation; his true *oikos* (home, household) focused on the here and now, envisioning afresh a world made new (the new reign of God).

His cultural context is largely dominated by the conditions arising from Roman occupation. Most people were poor and relied on the land for their survival. Excessive taxation proved a heavy burden for many and sometimes led to revolutionary groups, such as the Zealots. While Jesus was certainly a revolutionary in seeking to create an alternative empowering consciousness, he consistently adopted a nonviolent stance.

A second major cultural influence was that of Hellenization. The Greek language became the lingua franca of trade, commerce, and advanced education. Big cities such as Tiberias and Sepphoris, although constructed by the Romans, became epicenters of Greek culture and values. The Hellenization process began to overshadow the rural values and spiritual subtleties of the inherited Hebrew culture, even the literary nuances of the Aramaic language that Jesus spoke. Consequently, writing the Gospels in Greek undermined the native spirituality endemic to Jesus and his mission.

His public ministry was quite short—some claim as little as one calendar year—nonetheless long enough to make a significant cultural impact that roused suspicion and reaction among Romans and Jews. His empowering of the rank and file was what particularly irked the authorities. He was perceived as usurping their power and control, and when it came to his denunciation of the temple, the authorities (Roman and Jewish) knew they had to get rid of him. They did what they had done to several other subversives: crucified him on a cross.

Many of his male followers scattered, but others remained faithful, particularly a mixed group gathered around a woman called Mary from Magdala. Against heavy odds, this small, female-led group kept the prophetic flame alive, eventually laying the foundations for what was to become the church. In time that same church, now perverted by patriarchal domination, destroyed all evidence of the original founding group, replacing it with a reassembled male group based on the original twelve apostles.

From this overview, we glimpse an underlying archetype: Jesus as the *human face of God* made radically visible on earth. Toward the end of his comprehensive study on the archetypal significance of Jesus's humanity, Walter Wink (2002) concludes,

> If we claim that Jesus lived authentically, that he is exemplary, and that he is the human face of God; if we see in him the son of the man, and that he is the first-born of many sisters and brothers; if we assert that he was like us in every way, including being an imperfect, wounded, sinning human being—historiography can prove none of it. The myth of the human Jesus simply requires it. (251)

The Dispersed Prophetic Community

Our second epoch takes off around 33–35 CE and lasts till the mid 60s. Its primary driving force is Jesus's resurrection. Volumes have been written on this dimension, long assumed to be a miraculous resuscitation of a dead body. Today we tend to view it differently, as a transformative awakening among the early disciples whereby they felt Jesus to be more radically and really alive after his death than he had been even in his earthly life. The first beneficiaries of this mystic-type awakening were Mary Magdalene and her codisciples.

We tend to judge the first expansion of Christianity by the account in the Acts of the Apostles (compiled by St. Luke) and the supplementary vision and writings of Paul. According to Luke, the scattered group of twelve returned, now reconstituted with a new member called Matthias, and were missioned in the power of the Holy Spirit to spread the gospel. However, according to Acts, the spreading was done primarily by Peter and Paul, and to a lesser degree by James and Barnabas (who did not belong to the twelve). Their evangelization was mainly through preaching, teaching, and occasional miraculous deeds of healing. According to Acts and Paul's letters, this evangelization spread throughout Asia Minor, Greece, and westward as far as Rome.

This grandiose narrative needs supplementing with what was happening to people at the ground level. We can glean this from two references in Acts to the evolution of small communities that gathered for prayer, mutual support, and service to the poor and marginalized (see Acts 2:44–47; 4:32–37). It is now becoming much clearer that this communally empowering ministry arose from, and was focused on, the homestead (the *oikos*), with women as the primary catalysts in this unfolding grounding of faith and mission. This has never been formally recorded or acknowledged. Osiek and MacDonald (2006) provide a valuable overview.

From the authentic writings of St. Paul[1] we receive valuable insight into the egalitarian nature of this early epoch. First, we know that Paul was a Jew who never seems to have abandoned his Judaism, nor did he experience any conflict in integrating that faith with discipleship to Jesus. It seems that in Paul's time religious diversity and tolerance were widely adopted, thus allowing for a number of developmental stages in the incorporation of outsiders into the newly evolving fellowship. These outsiders are variously named as God-fearers, Gentiles, or Pagans.

Second, Paul himself seems to have collaborated closely with the female disciples and supported their empowering role in the growth and expansion of the Judeo-Christian community. Communal structures for fellowship and empowerment suggest that Paul is largely faithful to the gospel vision of the new reign of god, and leadership from the ground up is what Paul promotes and supports throughout many of his missionary journeys.

Third, despite the fact that Paul seems to have expected the end of the world during his lifetime (see 1 Thess. 4:13–18; 1 Cor. 7:31), and promoted an ascetical spirituality in preparation for it, he exhibits a pastoral integration transcending many of the dominating Greek dualisms of his time. As the foundational communities expand, Paul proposes an ecclesial orientation. Here he is

---

[1] Not all the letters that carry Paul's name belong to Paul. It was customary in early Christian times to adopt the name of a reputable person and attach it to another piece of writing in order to enhance its sales, even though the content might be substantially different from what the named source might author. Today we have to reckon with three Pauls, not merely one (see Borg and Crossan 2009). The authentic Paul is reflected in the letters to the Romans, Galatians, Philemon, Philippians, 1 Corinthians, and parts of 2 Corinthians. The second Paul is a much more conservative character who encourages slaves to obey their masters and wives to be subject to their husbands—in the disputed letters of Ephesians, Colossians, and 2 Thessalonians. The third is the reactionary Paul of 1 and 2 Timothy and Titus, tamed and co-opted by the values of the imperial culture, and quite antagonistic toward women; he holds very little resemblance to the original, authentic Paul.

adopting a political structure of his time (something akin to town or city council), which was reserved for males only. In adopting that structure, however, Paul insists that it must be open to females as well as to males.

Later Christendom conveys the notion that Paul's theology focused largely on the death and resurrection of Jesus, with no explicit references to the parables, miracles, or other features in the life of Jesus. How that affected his hearers is difficult to discern. It is his practical contribution to community egalitarian empowerment that concerns us primarily in the present work. It is at this level that we see Paul making a significant contribution to the early Christian community coming of age.

The Apocalyptic Shift

Our third period, approximately 65–100 CE, commences with a Jewish revolt that turned into a brutal suppression of the people of Israel, Jerusalem was raised to the ground, the temple was destroyed by fire, and an estimated one hundred thousand Jews were either killed or sold into slavery.

The destruction of the Second Temple in 70 CE marked a turning point in Jewish history. In the absence of the Temple, the synagogue became the center of Jewish life. When the Temple was destroyed, Judaism responded by fixating on the commandments of the Torah. Synagogues replaced the temple as a central meeting place, and the rabbis replaced high priests as Jewish community leaders. Because of the rabbis' dominance after 70 CE, the era is called the rabbinic period. The rabbis filled the void of Jewish leadership in the aftermath of the Great Revolt, and they created a new kind of Judaism through their literature and teachings.

For the embryonic Christian community (followers of the Way), it was a period of mixed fortunes. James Carroll (2014) claims that it was the Jewish-Roman War, more than anything else, that undermined the founding prerogative of Mary Magdalene and her colleagues, including Paul's foundational strand of egalitarian ecclesiology. In the pseudo-Pauline letters of Ephesians and Colossians we detect strands of disempowering stratification: slaves, obey your masters; wives, obey your husbands (Col. 3:22; Eph. 5:22–24; 6:5). By the time 1 and 2 Timothy came to be written (not by Paul, although they carry his name), female leadership within the emerging church is condemned to new patriarchal control, a move that would gather ever greater domination as centuries unfolded.

The orthodoxy of the new faith (followers of the Way) sought credibility in the power and prerogative of its male, patriarchal leadership, and a new ascetical spirituality enhanced the leadership in its attempt to exert domination and control. Realizing the antireligious tenor of the Roman conquerors, Christian leaders felt an urgent need to record the outstanding deeds of Jesus so that they could be preserved for posterity. This led to the writing of the Gospels, beginning with Mark around 70 CE.

Mark and the other evangelists were writing against the backdrop of the Great Jewish-Roman War (66–73), interpreting the challenge for Christians in terms of the apocalyptic vision of Daniel, Enoch, and others. A cult of martyrdom progressively came to the fore, and the earth-centered vision of Jesus, the anti-imperial kingdom of God, was eclipsed in favor of a renewed Israel in the eschatological age to come. This became the dominant focus for several generations of Christian leaders, and was strongly reinforced throughout the post-Constantinian era.

However, the research of recent times suggests that the emerging picture was a great deal more complex, with substantial differences between the rhetoric of the preachers and teachers and the organic, lived reality of the rank and file. The historical research of Brock and Parker (2008) highlights the fact that a spirituality of paradise on earth, rather than in a life hereafter, prevailed right into the eleventh century; even the martyrs associated with the Roman catacombs envisaged their death as a contribution to a better world in the here and now, rather than as an escape to a life hereafter.[2] An empowering faith in the Risen Christ, rather than a devotion of atonement, seems to have dominated the first Christian millennium.

This complex foundational picture marked a spiritual coming-of-age, which subsequent Christian history has poorly understood. Ecclesiastical power and domination persistently blinker our vision and distort the true story. In fact, I suspect that it is after the Council of Trent in the sixteenth century (1545–1563) that things took an ominous twist, with consequences that endure to the present time. From Trent onward the newly separated Catholic Church became a distinctive denomination, initiating a period of clerical domination, legalistic control, and a great deal of irrational fear in the face of any outside challenge. The distorted and dysfunctional coming-of-age that followed Trent morphed into four distinctive categories still visible today: *power, devotion, heresy,* and *altruism.*

Clericalized Power

Clerical power became a major issue at the Council of Trent, taking on a central importance also for the other denominations that emerged around the same time: Lutherans, Calvinists, and others. For Catholicism it was very much a panic reaction. Feeling embarrassed and shamed by the perceived betrayal of Protestantism, the Church resolved that it would do everything possible to ensure that such a departure from truth would never happen again.

To that end, Trent put in place a robust system of structure and regulation to safeguard the one and only truth, which the

---

[2] Throughout early Christendom, martyrdom tends to be viewed in honorific, exalted terms as the perennial witness in Christian discipleship. Such literature served a range of views, which are a great deal more complex than most commentators acknowledge. For a much more nuanced treatment, see the seminal work of historian Candida Moss (2013).

Catholic Church alone could deliver. To that end it created a superior person in charge, who is best described by four key words: male, white, celibate, and cleric.

- *Male.* Faithful to Aristotle's anthropology, endorsed by St. Thomas Aquinas, only males are considered to be full human beings, with God-given rational intelligence. The other half, females, cannot and must not be trusted with serious responsibilities for the future of the Church.
- *White.* At the time, the white Western world, which essentially means Europe, was considered to be the only civilized part of the planet. Colonization of other parts was already at work in the Americas and in subsequent centuries was to spread to other continents. The vision of Trent and colonization go hand in hand.
- *Celibate.* Since God was viewed as asexual, those who truly represent God must be asexual as well. But there is a further nuance to the celibate state, denoting a quality of holiness equal to God himself. The priest has been granted a divine (or at least semidivine) status.
- *Cleric.* Fundamentally, this means a quality of power equal to God himself. So, only a cleric is authorized to speak on God's behalf and to truly represent God on earth.

With this deadly combination—male, white, celibate, cleric— no prospect of coming-of-age is tolerated. Even the privileged clerical few cannot come of age, because they are ensconced in an idolatrous and tyrannical regime. Everybody ends up in codependent, dysfunctional relationships. In a sense everybody is powerless, in a system that eventually will implode. However, it can be so tightly buttressed that it can endure for centuries, eventually running out of energy, and fragmenting in a rather meaningless decimation. Evidence for this corrosive fragmentation is visible in all the Christian denominations today.

Popular Devotion

Those holding the power—the male, white, celibate clerics—enforced their power chiefly by perpetuating a form of devotionalism that kept people passive and feeling unworthy, obedient, and subservient. Such devotionalism flourished through various movements, one of the better known being that of Jansenism.[3] Original sin was highlighted as the central plight of all humanity, condemning humans to an enduring state of perversion and sin, which could only be remedied by penance and prayer, in the hope of making up to Jesus for his cruel sufferings (on the cross) caused by flawed humans.

One of the major problems with such devotions is that enough was never enough. The more penance one did, the more unworthy and inadequate one felt, so one always had to keep adding additional effort. Almost inevitably people began to internalize a tyrannical, demanding God that could never be satisfied, a God that would never give the graces necessary for salvation unless we bombarded him day and night.

Such intense pleading with this highly manipulative, punitive God was done through repetitive prayers (e.g., the Rosary), novenas, fasting and other forms of bodily deprivation, pilgrimages, exaggerated use of statues and holy pictures, and frequent attendance at church services. In this way, people were kept in perpetual childish immaturity, embracing a sense of faith with little or no sense of adult growth and development.

In the latter half of the twentieth century many people in the West outgrew the codependency of such devotionalism, and

---

[3] Named after a Dutch theologian, Cornelius Jansen (d. 1638), Jansenism was a distinct movement within the Catholic Church that flourished mainly in France in the seventeenth and eighteenth centuries. It strongly emphasized original sin, human depravity, the necessity of divine grace, and predestination. Although explicitly condemned by Popes Innocent X in 1653 and Clement XI in 1713, it was endorsed and supported by several Catholic leaders at the time and also influenced other Christian denominations.

in several cases abandoned Church practice completely. In other parts of the world, the devotions were integrated with popular fiestas and local community celebrations, and in that process the severity of the penitential practices was reduced significantly. In communities around the world, where poverty and violence prevail, such devotional practices are still prevalent as people hope against hope that God will intervene and rescue them from their awful situations. By upholding and encouraging such devotional practices, instead of confronting on a practical level the systemic injustice and oppression of such peoples, both church and state often collude in making the situation tolerable for the people. This will never lead to a responsible coming-of-age, and as I indicate in part 2 of this book, it is unlikely that Jesus would ever be satisfied with such a resolution.

Heresy and Monolithic Truth

In the post-Tridentine Church, any disagreement with, or deviation from, official Church teaching automatically put one outside the pale. There was no room for disagreement or for alternative opinion. There was no acknowledgment of the hugely diverse nature of faith in early Christian times. There was only one truth—and one way to knowing and appropriating truth—and that was through the teaching authority of the Catholic Church.

Theologians were merely mouthpieces for the hierarchy. Theology was strictly reserved to priests and those training for priesthood, a procedure that remained rigidly in place until the second half of the twentieth century. The grip began to loosen around 1970, when an estimated 5 percent of all theologians in the Catholic Church were laypeople; today, it is about 60 percent.

During the post-Tridentine period, heresy was not merely about deviating from right doctrine. More significantly, it denoted breaking the laws and rules in a Church becoming ever more preoccupied with law and canonical regulations, all leading up to the promulgation of the Code of Canon Law in 1917.

Law has always been a central feature of Christianity, but with a milder and less extensive application than what happened after the Council of Trent when a new legalistic momentum came into force, popularly known as the *Jus Novissimum* (newest law).

Marriage provides an interesting example. Before the Council of Trent, marriage was not a sacrament in the formal sense. There was a blessing of the union, and concern from the Church for the welfare of spouses and children, but a great deal was left to the people's own initiative in a culture characterized by trust and goodwill. After Trent we witness a gradual movement toward controlling every aspect of people's marital reality, to the present situation in which an estimated one-third of the Code of Canon Law is about marriage.

With more and more people coming of age, heresy is now largely reserved to the doctrinal sphere and the work of priest theologians (a rapidly decreasing subgroup). In several religious and spiritual contexts, laypeople (including nonclerics, such as Sisters) openly question, disagree with, and offer alternative viewpoints regarding official Church teaching. Truth is no longer seen as an ecclesiastical reserve. To the contrary, approximations to truth in the complex world of our time are deemed possible only through a process of multidisciplinary discernment (named in chapter 2 as *communal obedience*). As I indicate in part 2, this way of engaging truth seems far more congruent with the New Testament basis of our faith.

Altruism Indomitable

Despite all the negative factors outlined thus far, suggesting that the post-Tridentine period was one of regression and growing legalism, an incarnational altruism also thrived. Perhaps such a situation can remind us that despite cultural impositions from on high, a coming-of-age quality endures, particularly among those perceived to be the losers. In religious terms we note this in a range of countercultural movements flourishing throughout the post-Tridentine era.

On the religious front, one movement that has not received the attention it deserves is that of female religious congregations. In 1298 Pope Boniface VIII issued a decree, *Periculoso*, prescribing new and more rigorous standards for the enclosure of women religious than the Western Church had previously demanded. The bull reflected current fears that women were inherently passionate and lusted after sexual fulfillment even more ardently than men. At the Council of Vienne in 1311 Pope Clement V extended the *Periculoso* to include Beguines, Tertiaries, and other less formally consecrated women. At a later date Pope Pius V (1566–1572) declared solemn vows and strict papal enclosure to be essential to all communities of women religious. Such enclosure was never formally revoked, yet a new wave of female religious life emerged in the sixteenth and seventeenth centuries, with such pioneering figures as Angela Merici, Louise de Marillac, Mary Ward, and Mary MacKillop. They targeted the human and apostolic needs of the poor and marginalized, activating a range of services that were to evolve into the educational systems and health services we know today in many parts of the Western world.

Alongside the apostolic congregations of Sisters, a range of charitable services emerged, attending to the medical, social, and educational needs of people, particularly the very poor. Beyond a Church with a public ascetical and legalistic image, there flourished a widespread, active devotion, not focused on prayer and penance but on radiating the human face of Christ in compassionate love and empowering liberation. Few historical sources acknowledge this hidden coming-of-age, which sustained millions through pain and struggle.

Flourishing Rather than Surviving

While historians tend to record the outstanding accomplishments of heroic witnesses, mainly men, and their commanding management of people and resources, the deeper truth of Christian faith belongs to a more complex and largely hidden impetus pioneered by ordinary people, with women playing central roles. In early Christian times, even before Christianity outgrew its Jewish roots, ordinary women, through their homes and families, played significant roles. While the temple and the synagogue were largely controlled by males[4] and managed along patriarchal lines, the household (*oikos*) was characterized by female leadership and initiative. In rural Galilee, this is where the early synagogue meetings took place. It was in such households that Jesus often broke bread with his disciples, with women playing leading roles that in a few centuries would become a male preserve. The earliest expressions of Christian faith and flourishing took place in those households. Arguably, this is where Christianity came of age.

To counter the anti-Semitism that has marred Christianity from its earliest years, contemporary scholars seek to relocate Christian faith within its Jewish homestead. In some cases the argument goes so far as to suggest that Christianity should never have become a separate religion. Its original purpose (and that of the historical Jesus)—it is claimed—was to reform Judaism and not launch a new religion. Insofar, then, as Christianity did evolve as a new religion, it did so by betraying its true origins and maligning its mother faith as an inferior system populated by those who turned to false gods, away from the true path.

In the present work I argue that Christianity survived—and indeed flourished—as a world religion precisely because it outgrew its Judaic origins. Its coming-of-age required such a break. I fully support the view that we cannot understand the Christian faith, and the life and ministry of Jesus, without a thorough knowledge of their Jewish backgrounds. I also acknowledge that Jesus himself was a Jew, born and raised in that faith, as was St. Paul, who never converted to Christianity.

However, upholding the notion that Jesus was a Jew—living the religion fully throughout his life—and probably never desiring

---

[4] Bernadette Brooten (1982) provides some important information on female rabbis in pre-Christian and early Christian times.

a new religion in his name lacks evolutionary credibility. More-over, it smacks of the kind of projections that scholars too easily make. Traditionally, Scripture scholars have been chosen for their strong fidelity to faith (and church); all too easily they assume that Jesus would have been a similar faith-believer. In other words, they project onto the historical Jesus their own felt need for a strong religious foundation.

It strikes me that Jesus deviated on a large scale from his indigenous religion, not by way of rejecting it but by choosing to transcend it in favor of a more empowering spirituality. The para-bles and miracles speak to that alternative vision; their significance is explored in later chapters. And while the Sermon on the Mount frequently recalls the foundational Jewish sense of allegiance ("You have heard that it was said . . ."), Jesus is clearly pushing boundaries in the direction of an enlarged horizon of faith, as, for instance, in the command to love one's enemies (Matt. 5:43–44). Consequently, we must not hastily assume that the people would have envisaged Jesus primarily in a Jewish context. As Spanish theologian José Antonio Pagola (2009) boldly asserts,

> No one saw Jesus as a teacher devoted to explaining the religious traditions of Israel. They knew a prophet with a passion for a fuller life for everyone, who only wanted people to embrace God, so that God's reign of justice and mercy would become ever wider and more joyful. His goal was not to perfect the Jewish religion, but to hasten the coming of the long-awaited reign of God, which meant life, justice, and peace. (99)

Those who argue that Jesus as Messiah fulfills the older hopes and aspirations of the Jewish faith also get entangled in their own arguments. Over the centuries Christianity has invoked the mes-siahship of Jesus to justify the claim that Jesus has delivered in his life, death, and resurrection the liberation and deliverance that the Jewish people longed for but were never able to realize—a claim known as *supersessionism*. This rather derogatory dismissal of Judaism has been countered by several contemporary scholars (Jewish and Christian), who claim that the Christian notion of a messiah, particularly one who endures the rejection of his people and an ensuing barbaric death, is intolerable for a Jewish audience. In other words, such a Messianic figure is not congruent with Jewish hopes and expectations. Most scholars go on to add both an acceptance and endorsement of Jesus as an eminently prophetic person living out in an exemplary way the requirements of Torah and the covenant.

Thus, one contemporary Jewish scholar, Amy-Jill Levine (2007), writes,

> After two thousand years of ignorance, the time has come for church and synagogue, Jews and Christians, to understand our intertwined histories, to see Jesus as a Jew who made sense to other Jews in a Jewish context, to learn how our two traditions came to a parting of the ways, to recognize how misunderstandings of Jesus and Judaism continue even today to foster negative stereotypes and feed hate, and to explore how the gains in interfaith relations made over the past several decades can be nurtured and expanded. (16)

Nonetheless, later in the same book, Levine (2007) remarks, "Had the church remained a Jewish sect, it would not have achieved its universal mission. Had Judaism given up its particularistic practices, it would have vanished from history. That the two movements eventually separated made possible the preservation of each" (84). Every evolutionary breakthrough entails, to one degree or another, a rupture from its "parent" model. In human developmental terms, the teenager or young adult needs to leave the family nest to have any realistic hope of becoming adult in her or his own right.

The ensuing challenge is that of discerning between what we should retain from the past and what we should outgrow and transform (evolution always moves in the direction of greater complexity). One major challenge here is the phenomenon of violence in Judaism and Christianity. A popular biologist, Richard Dawkins, is well known for his antireligious rhetoric. Nevertheless, few can deny the veracity of his critique of the Hebrew Scriptures when Dawkins writes (2006), "The God of the Old Testament is arguably the most unpleasant character in all fiction: jealous and proud of it; a petty, unjust, unforgiving control-freak; a vindictive, bloodthirsty ethnic cleanser; a misogynistic, homophobic, racist, infanticidal, genocidal, filicidal, pestilential, megalomaniacal, sadomasochistic, capriciously malevolent bully" (31).

Jesuit scholar Raymond Schwager (1987) uses much more subdued language while still highlighting a disturbingly violent portrayal of God: "The Hebrew Bible contains 1,000 verses where God's own violent actions of punishment are described, 100 passages where Yahweh expressly commands others to kill people, and several stories where God kills or tries to kill for no apparent reason. Violence is easily the most often mentioned activity and central theme of the Hebrew Bible" (60).[5]

This violent undercurrent features in every major world religion, whether intentionally or not. And while recent scholarship strives to reclaim the foundational nonviolent meaning of Jesus and the Gospels (cf. Rynne 2008; Neufeld 2011; Trocmé 2014), the history of Christianity exhibits no shortage of religious violence. Jesus, who champions a nonviolent way, strikes me as one who marks a significant departure from how God is portrayed throughout the Hebrew Scriptures. He not merely brings to fulfillment what was endemic to his own faith tradition, he transcends and supersedes it in a whole new way.

In this regard, Christians face an enormous coming-of-age. Confronted with such a lurid history of violence—within and

---

[5] In reference to violence in the Gospels, Thomas Yoder Neufeld (2011) offers the following overview: "Matthew is seen as particularly vengeful, Luke as an apologist of the Roman Empire, and John as dangerously dualistic and anti-Semitic" (17).

without—how do we reclaim the nonviolent Jesus, and what would the ensuing discipleship look like in the violent twenty-first century? I respond to that challenge in part 2.

What Survival Will Entail

Yes, Christianity will survive—and even thrive—as we move deeper into the twenty-first century, but not without some drastic changes. The following are some of the critical issues we've reviewed briefly in the present chapter:

- Making the shift from power to empowerment.
- Outgrowing the ideological clericalism of the Council of Trent.
- Re-creating a church of the people, shifting the focus away from hierarchy and clergy.
- Making devotions and prayer structures more congruent with a theology of flourishing.
- Outgrowing child-parent codependency in favor of adult faith maturity.
- Expanding the Christian-Jewish connection into the sphere of multifaith dialogue.
- Adopting a radical option for nonviolent discipleship.
- Bringing earth and all creatures into the relational matrix of our faith.

These challenges call us to move beyond the anthropocentrism that has stultified our vision for too long. Christianity, in terms of its seminal vision of the new reign of God (more in chapter 6), is not merely about human beings, and even less so about the exclusive realm of the human soul. Jesus operated out of a large cosmic view, embracing every creature with which we share the web of life. I outline and explain this enlarged horizon in part 2.

Part Two

Revisioning Our Christian Story

Literalism, rationalism, and spiritualism are among Christianity's greatest distractions. The Gospels undoubtedly preserved a cherished memory of Jesus and even how he was remembered by people of his day. Nonetheless, those memories are filtered through a range of cultural, social, and religious norms. Even the journalistic standards of the time were significantly different from ours, with far less emphasis on the kind of objective data modern readers require. Nothing in the Gospels—probably in the entire Bible— can be taken literally. Poetry rather than prose, metaphor rather than objective statement, the symbolic rather than the rational— all provide more reliable pathways to the underlying truth.

The kind of rationality that characterizes the post-Enlightenment era (since the early 1800s) has roots in the Greek metaphysics and epistemology that were invading the world in which Jesus lived. However, not until the fourth century (and thereafter) did Constantine seek to establish Christianity on a solid doctrinal basis—to which all inhabitants of the empire would submit—and did rationalism begin to dictate the direction of Christian teaching. Mystery was credible to the extent that it could be couched in the logic of Greek philosophy (from which Scholasticism duly emerged) and developed under the vigilant eye of patriarchal guardians.

Inevitably a two-tier system began to unfold, the fuller impact of which is more notable at the Council of Trent (1545–1563). Truth was entrusted to the male, white, celibate cleric; he and he alone could speak for God, and only the cleric had full access to divine holiness. The masses were deemed to be spiritually unenlightened and were to depend totally on their priests for spiritual (sacramental) guidance. The people colluded, simultaneously developing a range of popular devotions to satisfy both their emotional and spiritual thirst. It was often a spirituality devoid of creative theology (hence, the notion of spiritualism), but what made it really deviant was not what the people were doing but the manner in which ecclesiastical powers promoted and encouraged such devotional practices in order to cow people into submission.

The sturdy patriarchal edifice, with literalism, rationalism, and spiritualism among its solid foundations, endured shaky moments at various times in history—for example, in the high Middle Ages, when feminism and creation spirituality were flourishing. In our time not merely did the foundations shake, they actually began to disintegrate—from 1960 onward. A charismatic fervor of music, dance, and song rattled the solemn tenor of the inherited rational mood. Many people walked away and no longer felt guilty. Others moved into the domain of sacred learning and began to access the onetime closed world of Scripture, theology, and morality. Everything was up for question.

In the complex landscape of the twenty-first century we inhabit an amorphous and highly diverse religious environment. Public media often highlight people or movements that no longer believe and support the practice of religion, such as the so-called new atheism (traditionally associated with the late Christopher Hitchens, Richard Dawkins, and Daniel Dennett). Many people describe themselves as spiritual but not religious; some say they still believe in God, but not the one they accepted in their youth;

and millions around the world are still fascinated by the Jesus of Christianity.

Which brings us to the material in part 2 of this book. The Jesus who fascinates and engages people in the twenty-first century embodies a very different reality from what we have known throughout much of Christendom. The attractive lure is in his radical humanity rather than his imperial divinity; in his subversive, empowering storytelling rather than in metaphysically couched dogmas; and in the liberative and empowering vision of his expansive horizon (called the kingdom of God in the Gospels) rather than in affiliation to any church, sect, or denomination. A morbid fascination with his untimely death (such as in Mel Gibson's gory narrative, *The Passion of the Christ*) gives way to justice-based solidarity with his prophetic contestation of the reigning powers. Salvation and redemption become a human responsibility in fidelity to the empowering imperative for which Jesus gave his life even to the point of death. Finally his resurrection is celebrated in all who rise from the depths of despair, incarnating a hope that helps to bring about heaven on earth.

The implications of this daring prophetic vision—and the ensuing call to come of age in embracing its deliverance—become the basis of our reflections in part 2.

5

History and Archetype

Where Do We Begin?

Jesus is very deliberately trying to short-circuit that grasping, acquiring, clinging, comparing linear brain and to open up within us a whole new mode of perception, not what we see, but how we see, how the mind makes its connections. This is a classic strategy of a master of wisdom.

—Cynthia Bourgeault

A messiah complex, however virtuous, is a formula for burnout. . . . The messianic age remains always yet to come in history; it is not a literal time-to-come, but an ideal that resists every realized eschatology.

—Catherine Keller

What came to be known as the Christian canon of Scripture was first established around the end of the fourth century. Pope Damasus's commissioning of the Latin Vulgate edition of the Bible around 383 CE was instrumental in finalizing the canon in the West. The Council of Carthage (397 CE), overseen by St.

Augustine, regarded the canon as already closed. Prior to that time a diversity of views prevailed on several key features of the newly emerging faith, acknowledging that the fourfold structure of the Gospels had prevailed since the late second century, as Hill (2010) highlights. From the fourth century on, with Christianity approved as the formal religion of the Roman world, the notion of a fixed text—with an accompanying rigidity of doctrine—became widely accepted and remained largely uncontested until the twentieth century.

A literal interpretation of Scripture became normative, reflecting a divine imperial mandate of a God that could not err, and whose one true nature could be revealed only to those designated by the imperial Church to be the interpreters of such truth. The Latin Vulgate became the foundational source, and remained so until the mid-twentieth century. Protestant scholars from the nineteenth century onward raised serious questions about this monolithic approach, particularly as related to the historical Jesus.[1] And with the promulgation of *Divino Aflante Spiritu* (Inspired by the Holy Spirit) by Pope Pius XII in 1943, Catholic scholars received a new mandate to probe ancient sources predating the Vulgate. The task of Gospel interpretation received a novel impetus, the consequences of which continue to the present. With hindsight, we can assert that Christian discernment of Scripture embraced a new coming-of-age in the mid-twentieth century.

Research into the historical Jesus has been a major thrust of this scriptural revival. Three major quests have been identified.[2]

---

[1] Most historians credit Samuel Reimarus (1694–1768) as the person who initiated the quest for the historical Jesus. Reimarus's *Fragments* was published posthumously by G. E. Lessing from 1774 to 1778. In it Reimarus sharply distinguished between the *Jesus of history* and the *Christ of faith*. In the late eighteenth and nineteenth centuries, many attempts were made at reconstructing a historical portrait of Jesus, including those of Karl F. Bahrdt, Karl H. Venturini, Martin Kahler, and D. F. Strauss. William Wrede and Albert Schweitzer are two of the key names bringing this research into the twentieth century.

[2] The first quest tends to be dated from the late 1700s up to 1953,

Meanwhile, the popularizing of the distinction between the Jesus of history and the Christ of faith (largely associated with Rudolf Bultmann) remains a foundational touchstone for the truth of our faith. History can only unravel so much—in fact, relatively little. The story of Jesus, it transpires, is not so much about historical fact as about a transcendent vision that evokes awe and admiration, and compels discipleship at various levels.

Divine and Human

American writer James Carroll (2014) strongly declared Jesus to be fully divine:

> What can that mean now? . . . If Jesus were not regarded as God almost from the start of his movement, he would be of no interest to us. We would never have heard of him. Nothing but his divinity accounts for his place in Western culture—or in my heart. . . . Nothing but a two-thousand-year-old divinity claim puts Jesus before us today. . . . And finally, the truest argument—not proof—for the divinity of Jesus is in the one undenied fact of this history: that billions upon billions of ordinary human beings have found in this faith an immediate and saving experience of the real presence of God, "partaking" of God—becoming God. (12, 279)

Despite this cogently argued conviction, particularly as Carroll (like several modern scholars) wishes to relocate Jesus in his indigenous Jewish context, Carroll (2014) also concedes that "*Modern belief and critical disbelief both seem compelled to*

---

the date usually cited for the launch of the second quest. The third quest, launched in the 1980s, aimed at an agreed set of criteria (e.g., multiple attestation, dissimilarity, embarrassment) to establish historicity, while also employing insights from a range of other disciplines, such as archaeology and ancient history.

choose between Jesus either as a human, complete with sinfulness like every other human, or as God uniquely immune from fallibility. But those who gave us the only portraits we have of Jesus seem not to have been torn by this contradiction, which is why their witness is so elusive" (257).

✳

Personal Reflection

I have deliberately italicized the above quotation because it so clearly articulates one of the major challenges I seek to explore in the present work: What might an archetypal interpretation of Jesus look like? Is the archetypal and the divinity one and the same or are they different (which, I suggest, they are), and wherein does the difference lie? At a more personal level, the quote also captivates much of my own faith journey, from a childlike dependence on, and fear of, a powerful divine figurehead above the sky, to a growing suspicion—initially awakening in my early twenties—that there is to this same God figure a deeply human dimension that believers must reconcile. In my student years I was richly blessed to have discovered the inspired writings of a then-Jesuit priest and theologian, Ladislaus Boros (d. 1981), whose attempt at a Christian anthropology lured me into exploring the meaning of Jesus as the human face of God made radically visible on earth.

That understanding grew ever deeper in my heart and became the lynchpin of my Christian theology. Gradually I began to realize that much of the doctrinal emphasis on the divinity of Jesus was used to cow believers into submission and obedience to the patriarchal church. Instead of being the basis for a mature and empowering adult faith, it kept people locked into an unhealthy codependence. More importantly, my growing familiarity with the story of Jesus, as it became insinuated into my own faith journey, was persuading me—intellectually and spiritually—that for me as a Christian it was the humanity of God in Jesus that I needed to come to terms with, not his divinity. At times, all the focus on Jesus's divinity felt like a gross distraction from that radical new way of being human revealed in the historical Jesus's life and ministry.

So what was this radical new way of being human, and what made it so alluring? It was the transpersonal context embodied in the gospel notion of the kingdom of God, which I outline in the next chapter. It took me several years to salvage Jesus from the anthropocentric construct purported by Greek anthropology (and translated into Scholasticism), depicting a robust, heroic, isolated, rational individual (the buffered self), instead of the more relational embodiment that I was gradually discovering at the heart of my evolving faith. Particularly difficult about this process was explaining to others what was awakening within and around me. Our entire modern world is so indoctrinated in Greek anthropology, or its neo-Darwinian derivatives, that making sense of what I was discovering is almost impossible. In fact it continues to be a major challenge, the fuller implications of which become clearer throughout the subsequent chapters of this book.

Two other comments on the quote from James Carroll: First, the early followers of Jesus do not seem to have been "torn by this contradiction," namely, the distinction between the humanity and divinity of Jesus. In other words, the early Christians were able to integrate these seemingly opposite characteristics, because they had access to a quality of creativity and imagination that our excessively rationalized world has subverted, and in some cases crushed completely. I think that Scripture scholar John Dominic Crossan (1996) gets it absolutely right in this witty and oft-quoted passage: "My point, once again, is not that those ancient people told literal stories and we are now smart enough to take them symbolically, but that they told them symbolically and we are now dumb enough to take them literally" (79). This literalism has caused untold damage to the growth and evolution of Christian faith.

Second, when Carroll claims that "their witness is so elusive," I suspect his own rationalism is getting in the way of a deeper truth. Employing creativity and imagination at a symbolic level that defies so much of our rationality and literalism, our ancient ancestors were already delving into the depths of archetypal meaning long before the notion was defined and described in the contemporary social sciences. Their witness is elusive to our rational modality but not to that mystical/archetypal realm that transcends dualistic splitting, and challenges us to see the deep interconnectedness that in our time quantum physics is rediscovering. At this level there is no rational distinction between humanity and divinity. Mystery reveals to us what is ultrareal.

❅

When James Carroll (2014) claims that human beings are capable of having "an immediate and saving experience of the real presence of God, 'partaking' of God—becoming God" (279), that experience must not be explored and discerned just within one modality (understanding God as divine), but must be kept open for a range of interpretative possibilities. Modern commentators from various disciplinary backgrounds highlight the complex nature of human experience and the several influences that require focused and persistent discernment. Kathleen Lyons (2015) highlights a number of these complexities.

To begin with, there is the face-value judgment that prevailed over several Christian centuries identifying the transcendent dimension of God to be one with the divine aspect, dualistically opposed and superior to the human aspect. The divinity was persistently exonerated in Jesus as the Christ, frequently identified with Jesus as Messiah. In this context, the powerful divinity is what really mattered, not the human dimension. From around 1960 onward the pendulum swung very much in the opposite direction, with a gradual appropriation of Jesus's humanity as the foundational truth of what Christians call *incarnation*, with Jesus viewed as a radical human embodiment of God's presence on earth, as I explore at greater length elsewhere (O'Murchu 2017).

Various attempts have been made to transcend the split between the divine and human in the revelation of God through the life and ministry of Jesus. This attempt at integration has been inspired for a variety of interpretative reasons, including the claim that in the ancient Hebrew (Jewish) culture, the Hellenistic desire for dualistic clarity was unknown. Additionally, insights from anthropology, psychology, and sociology provide further possibilities for a more integrated approach.

No single model of integration has won widespread approval. In fact, Jesus studies today are marked by a huge divergence of scholarly opinion, desired by some in the name of postmodern fluidity, and condemned by others as reckless relativism. While acknowledging such diversity, and not wishing to impose yet another dominant metanarrative, I offer a synthesis conducive to the evolutionary wisdom embraced by wise elders in our time. It hinges on the Jungian notion of the archetypal and was adopted by the late Walter Wink as his contribution to a more empowering Christology for the twenty-first century (see Wink 2002).

Toward an Archetypal Jesus

Introducing the archetypal approach, Wink writes (2002), "The interminable debates about the two natures of Christ seem to me totally off the mark. They strike me as an irrelevancy carried over from a worldview that for many is now defunct" (30). He goes on to highlight how the archetypal significance of Jesus is not a mere transcendent quality but one grounded in an evolutionary epicenter at a specific moment in time: "When Jesus appeared on the scene, the collective unconscious of the age was fully prepared. His life tapped into the massive psychic upheaval that was affecting numerous groups, not merely in Judaism, but in the Mediterranean world generally. Something seismic was about to happen, and Jesus stood at the epicenter" (2002, 65).

Describing the archetypal nature of Jesus as the Human Being (with capital letters), Wink (2002) continues,

> The Human Being is more than simply Jesus; it represents the future of all humanity, indeed, the world, in the purposes of God (Rom. 8:18–25). Then, during his Galilean mission, Jesus could at times virtually identify with the Human Being (while, occasionally, including his disciples as well) because it was Jesus who was primarily incarnating the Human Being and using it as an image of transformation. . . . As an archetype, the Human Being also mediates the possibility of becoming more human in the image and likeness of God, the Humane One. The Human Being is a catalytic agent for transformation, providing the form, lure and hunger to become what we are meant to be. . . . Most important perhaps, Jesus shows us something of what it means to be human, but not enough to keep us from having to discover our own humanity. We must weave the story, and for each of us the story will be unique. . . . The early Christians had the clear sense that the Human Being is not restricted to Jesus, but that it is an authority they are permitted to assume for themselves. (193, 139, 78)

This résumé of Walter Wink's empowering Christology is centered around two key notions:

- The primary identity of God working in and through the historical Jesus is of an archetypal nature, and that archetypal intent becomes manifest primarily in the humanity of Jesus.
- While embracing all that is genuine in the ordinariness of the human condition (including fragility and "sinfulness"), there is an extraordinariness, which in Wink's own words provides "the form, lure and hunger to become what we are meant to be." This transformative capacity requires a fundamental reexamination of what we understand by human personhood.

First, a human person is not a mere biological organism, ensouled or otherwise. It is not our biological substance or genetic makeup that defines our identity, nor is it the religious assertion that we are enlivened by a soul. Second, our personal identity does not end with our skin, the outer horizon by which each of us is visibly identified as a unique person. Third, what constitutes our personal uniqueness is a great deal more than Aristotle's suggested capacity for rational thought.

The Human Archetype

What, then, does it mean to be authentically human? In archetypal terms, what constitutes our human makeup? *Relationality* is a central concept.[3] We are relational beings, and relationship is

---

[3] It is also a central theological concept that has been given short shrift. In his overview of Trinitarian theology, Richard Rohr (2016, 44–45) notes that the Church resolved the doctrinal debate on the nature of the threesome God by employing the notion of a subsistent relationship. The relational dimension was affirmed but the distinctive substance of each of the three persons is to be upheld, and throughout much of Christianity's history it is the individuality of the threesome rather than their relational status that prevailed. For a more philosophical approach to human relationality, MacKenzie and Stoljar (2000)

the driving force in our coming-into-being and in everything that transpires within and around us over the span of a lifetime—and indeed beyond our earthly horizon.

Ours is a psychic rather than merely a biological existence. *Psyche* normally denotes a combination of mind and spirit, emphasizing the transphysical (biological) foundational truth of who we really are as persons. Psyche also essentially denotes energy, the foundational reality of everything in the universe, but to be understood in terms of quantum theory (see chapter 3 above) rather than in classical science where energy tends to be defined in terms of function and human usefulness. Psychic energy is the driving force of Spirit, a primordial life force that might be described as an envelope of consciousness informing creation since time immemorial. This inspirited energy cannot be reduced to any one religious belief or to all the great religions put together. It predates them all, back into the realms of deep time.

The archetypal human, therefore, is first and foremost an energy being—or, more accurately, an energy-becoming. This energy identity can be gleaned from the image on the next page.

We look at people in their physical biological outlines, and we assume that their identity corresponds to what we can see and observe. But that is merely the anthropocentric/physical outline of a human body and the external manifestation of a human personality. As indicated in the images on the next page, around each of our bodies are various layers of energy. That nearest our skin is called the *aura,* which extends six or eight inches from the body. Expanding outward is a sequence of other energy layers or fields—in all, six or seven, according to esoteric medicine. These energy waves are not merely an integral dimension of who and what we are (becoming); they are essential to our existence and human flourishing. Without them we would not even exist.

---

provide a valuable overview. The implications for our understanding of human personhood are described by Bernd Oberdorfer and Michael Welker in their respective contributions to the compendium *The Work of the Spirit* (Welker 2006).

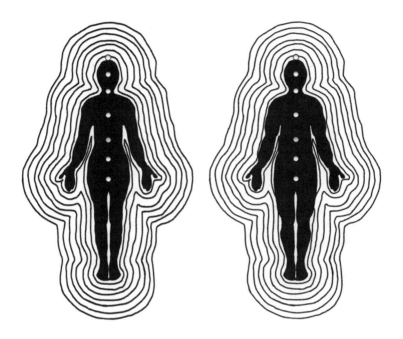

As we each approach the end of life, as death is imminent, the energy fields begin to disappear—from the outside inward. The aura is the last to leave, and then the physical body ceases to function, but *our energy selves are still more real and enduring than our physical bodies.* Even more significant is what happens to our energy selves after death. We know from conventional science that energy is never destroyed; it is converted into other energy forms. The energy that was constellated in my individual being during my earthly existence is reconfigured within the great energy fields of creation at large. I continue to coexist at another level of creation.[4]

The human is not so much the outcome of biological reproduction as that of a generic evolutionary process. My coming into

---

[4] Some people are quick to jump to the conclusion that I am embracing the notion of reincarnation. Not quite. Nor am I consciously endorsing the Christian notion of resurrection (from the dead).

the world is based on an energy awakening, overtly experienced in the mutual attraction of my parents for one another.[5] As this attraction becomes ever more eroticized, a range of creative urges awaken, of which the desire to procreate is just one. While the process of birthing new life can be explained biologically, covertly a range of cosmic and planetary energies are being activated and employed. Strictly speaking my parents are mediators rather than causes of a procreative process. (Cause and effect cannot fully explain what is happening at the quantum level.)

People often talk casually about a child coming into the world, an understanding that belongs mainly to dysfunctional religion. We each come *out of the world*; we don't come into it. Every human, as already stated, is born out of the relational matrix through which everything in creation grows and flourishes. Moreover, we bring with us, in the deep inner psyche, the dreams and aspirations endemic to creation at large. In more authentic religious terms, we are spirit-beings (more accurately, spirit-becomings), offspring of that divine/cosmic creativity that indigenous people all over our world name as the Great Spirit.

I am describing here some of the underlying features of the human archetype. As outlined in chapter 3, Carl Jung claimed that the archetypes emanate from the collective unconscious, which he understood as a kind of envelope of creative energy containing the whole creation. Although Jung made some brief allusions to quantum physics, he never explored the deeper connections I outline above. Jung's familiarity with quantum physics is extensively covered by Paul Levy (2018). He also considered the collective unconscious to have spiritual significance, of a quality transcending the

---

[5] Where the interaction is mutually erotic and followed through on a shared commitment, then this theory is intelligible. In the case of a forced pregnancy (lacking in mutual consent, rape), then it is more difficult to uphold the argument. Nonetheless, a foundational truth of the human search for meaning underpins the argument, despite the negative outcome that happens at times.

formal religions known to humankind. For Jung, the archetype can manifest in the life of any person and tends to do so in our more creative moments, or through the complex realm of our dreams and fantasies.

What Jung failed to consider was how the human archetype manifests at a cultural level in a range of more highly evolved persons. The mystics probably provide a more authentic expression of this phenomenon—people who evoke in others awakenings and aspirations after a quality of wholeness that is never fully attainable but forever haunts and lures us. Volumes have been written on the meaning and cultural significance of mysticism, frequently described in overly idealized religious terms. In archetypal terms, the split between religious and nonreligious makes no sense. The archetypal integration, transcending the distinction between religious and non-religious, is evidenced in the lives of inspiring people such as Nelson Mandela, Rosa Parks, Mahatma Ghandi, and Martin Luther King Jr.

We can now offer a brief résumé of the outstanding features that constitute the human archetype:

- One who brings the creative energy of the universe to a new, empowering transparency.
- One who evidences in one's life a compelling sense of transcendent meaning.
- One whose entire mode of being (and behavior) is living proof that we inhabit a universe where relationality is the primordial orientation of all that exists.
- One who recapitulates and embodies for our contemporary world something of the rich and complex development our species has undergone throughout the 7 million years of our human evolutionary story.
- One who seems to be endowed with a deeper capacity for integrating light and shadow. While perhaps heroic in some ways, this person can also present as a fragile human being prone to human error and sin.

- One for whom the pursuit of rationality is of secondary concern, with intuition, imagination, and the creative urge being at the fore.
- One whose foundational identity transcends the cultural dictates of nationality, ethnicity, and religious allegiance.

Jesus as an Archetypal Human

We now move on to consider Jesus as an archetypal person and to reexamine the Christian story from that perspective. Over the centuries, Christians have been doing this in their descriptions of Jesus as *the Christ*. In biblical and theological terms, the title is used in reference to Jesus as Messiah, the divine embodiment of God's rulership over all life. However, the word *messiah* carries a range of other connotations, often vaguely described to denote a transhuman or superhuman identity for the historical Jesus. The term *cosmic Christ* has been used for two somewhat contradictory purposes: (1) the imperial claim that Jesus is God's only true representative ruler for all humankind (indeed, for all creation), thus insinuating that Christianity is superior to all other forms of religion; and (2) an attempt at religious inclusivity, whereby the historical Jesus is unique for Christians, but as the Christ embodies the aspirations and hopes for deeper meaning encountered throughout the entire human species.

Additionally, there is a personalist understanding of the attribution to Jesus as "the only Son of the Father," depicted in John's Gospel as always doing what the Father wishes. In this interpretation, Father and Son are often endowed with excessive anthropocentric significance, inescapably favoring and exalting the superior status of the male gender, but also unwittingly employing an understanding of personhood that belongs more to Greek anthropology rather than to God or Jesus.

It seems to me that the title of "the Christ" is better understood as an attempt at articulating and honoring Jesus's archetypal nature. However, the term is so overloaded with historical baggage—patriarchal, imperial, religiously exclusive, excessively anthropocentric—it is probably not a useful or responsible title anymore. Moreover, as Lorraine Parkinson (2015) and other contemporary scholars claim, it is unlikely that the historical Jesus himself ever claimed the honorific title. Even though we find it in the New Testament, its historical context of rulership and patriarchal domination probably belong to the long imperial tradition that began with Constantine.

However, I am committed to reworking the tradition, not merely discarding it as useless or irrelevant. As such, my attempted reconstruction begins with the imperial, royal material, taking my initial inspiration from the archetypal analysis of Walter Wink (2002): "The Human Being must be corporate to further the human project, because we cannot become human by ourselves. We are inseparably social. Individuation is not individualism. We are one body, not just as a church, but as a species" (210).

I also remind the reader of an elusive phrase that occurs in the writings of the late Marcus Borg (1994a; 1994b): the community that *is* Jesus (emphasis mine). As archetypal humans we can never access the fuller and deeper meaning of Jesus solely by focusing on his individual human personhood, which Christendom has done for most of two thousand years. Jesus represents something much bigger, deeper, and more mysterious. The Gospels describe it as the kingdom of God (or of heaven, in Matthew's Gospel). It is the exploratory material for our next chapter and the first major step at reclaiming Jesus as the archetypal human.

Beyond Conventional Assumptions

Consequently, we need to outgrow several inherited attributions that we have employed in establishing an identity for Jesus. I have already alluded to the human projections we use in defining and describing Jesus's divinity. The all-powerful, all-knowing God that Jesus represents is essentially a cultural stereotype of the God that our patriarchal ancestors desired, and the one still favored by those millions who view and connect with God in a codependent fashion. Perhaps the more authentic way to engage with the divinity of Jesus is through that mystical notion of the *apophatic*, which basically denotes the less said, the better; only silence is likely to reveal to us the deeper meaning of the divine.

A related factor—an interpretative tool rather than an assumption—is the messianic identity attributed to Jesus. Walter Wink (2002) offers the following cultural context, providing a useful backdrop to the felt need for a divine messianic rescuer:

> The world that Jesus entered was seething with human longings that showed in messianic dreams, millennial fantasies, apocalyptic desperation, mystical revelations, suicidal nationalism, religious critique and reform, reactionary rigidity, and a sense that time was collapsing, that the future was foreshortened, that the mystery of reality was about to be revealed. In such a milieu, the authenticity of Jesus was like a beacon that drew all mythological motifs to itself. Incubating in the womb of that period was God's rash gamble that humanity might become more humane. (250)

Before the Roman invasion in 63 BCE, the land of Israel was occupied by several warring factions, all enjoying temporary periods of domination and control. Canaan had significant geopolitical importance till 1250 BCE when political upheaval struck, demolishing cities and dispersing the populace. After a period of restoration by successive kings—Saul, David, Solomon—the kingdom eventually split in two, with Israel to the north and Judah to the south.

Exile is a recurring theme throughout the Hebrew Scriptures. The first major exile is that of the Israelites of the northern kingdom (Samaria) carried out by the Assyrians. It occurred in two phases, first in 734 BCE under Tiglath-pileser III (2 Kgs. 15:29) and then, in 722 BCE, under Shalmaneser and his successor, Sargon II, when the city of Samaria was destroyed and the northern kingdom ceased to exist (2 Kgs. 17:5–6). The next major exile involved the destruction of the southern kingdom (Judah) and the city of Jerusalem. It, too, took place in several phases, all under the Babylonian king Nebuchadnezzar II (Jer. 52:28–30)—the worst being in 586 BCE (Jer. 52:29), when Solomon's temple was destroyed and the dynasty of David came to an end.

In one sense the Babylonian exile of the sixth century ended when King Cyrus of Persia issued an edict in 538 BCE, allowing the exiled Jews to return to Jerusalem and rebuild their city and the temple. This was viewed as an affirmation of Jeremiah's prophesy that the exile would end after seventy years (Jer. 25:11–12; 29:10–11) and was heralded by Isaiah's call that all exiles should return to the homeland (48:20). Exile, however, took on another significance, namely, a sense of spiritual separation from Yahweh; consequently, geographical return alone would not resolve the felt estrangement. Indeed, a number of texts from the later Second Temple period, among them the book of Daniel and 4 Ezra, understood the exile to endure for many subsequent centuries, with the people still awaiting deliverance from bondage.

What exactly was this bondage that dictated such a persistent religious ideology? The historical details have been extensively documented, and much of the relevant information can be accessed online. However, the cultural/religious interpretation is extremely complex, with an enduring sense of alienation and guilt around human failure in relation to God, and God's prospective threat of punishment for such enduring infidelity. In the face of this dilemma, the notion of a messiah comes into play. Only God could rescue the people from the exile and alienation they had known for so long. Moreover, only a powerful, kinglike deity could bring about such release. King David became the historical ideal to fulfill that role, with an impact that endured into New Testament times.

The messianic expectation, therefore, is interwoven with a quality of codependency that is endemic to patriarchal power and governance. The underlying script goes something like this: God has so designed the world that those who rule from on high have privileged access to the supreme ruling God. This hierarchical chain of command forever seeks to rope into line—into faithful obedience—wayward humans, and all humans are fundamentally flawed. What's more, humans themselves have internalized this codependency with a collective sense of guilt somewhat akin to children who feel that they can never measure up to harsh parental demands.

Patriarchal religion makes tough demands but tries to convince the wayward, codependent humans that these demands are ultimately based on love—once again reminiscent of harsh parents trying to convince their children that they are being punished for their own good. At the end of this convoluted process, humans are exhausted, and God is exasperated. God tries one last desperate ploy, sending his own beloved one to be a sacrifice (i.e., a scapegoat) that will reverse the messy, age-long situation and reassure the codependent juniors that they stand a better chance of winning God's good favor, although they will still never get it fully right.

Sending the messianic liberator is not a matter of theological difference between Jews and Christians. It is a narrative based on a long history of internalized oppression, and the proposed patriarchal resolution only adds further layers of debilitating anomie and powerlessness. Neither the Gods nor the humans stand any chance in terms of coming-of-age. Arguably all of the great religions, in terms of their deep script, offer a more coherent resolution capable of facilitating the coming-of-age I am describing.[6] Historically, however, this deeper wisdom has rarely come to the surface; too much patriarchal baggage consistently undermines and dislodges the more liberating vision.

---

[6] Notions like the covenant in the Hebrew Scriptures and the kingdom of God in the Christian Gospels seem to embody the deeper, more empowering wisdom to which I am alluding.

Salvation as Human Breakthrough

This religious ideology, vested in the rescuing power of the ruling God, evolved out of a set of patriarchal projections in which the patriarchs tried to mold God in their own image and likeness. Idolatry, and not exile, is at the root of *our* problem. Divinity, therefore, is endowed with elaborate, extraordinary power, leaving humans powerless, estranged, and with little option other than to throw themselves at the mercy of this all-powerful, redemptive, divine rescuer. In this process, humans lose all meaningful connection with the organic web of life, being persuaded by patriarchal religion that their best hope is to seek escape from this sin-infected vale of tears. Earthlings have been uprooted and exiled, not because of original sin or any other type of fundamental flaw but because of patriarchal religion itself. Coming-of-age is impossible in this situation.

How do we break the chains of this inherited bondage? How do we transcend the codependency in which we have been trapped for centuries? One remarkable passage from the encyclical letter of Pope Francis, *Laudato Si'*, offers an important lifeline: "Nature cannot be regarded as something separate from ourselves, or as a mere setting in which we live. We are part of nature, included in it and thus in constant interaction with it" (no. 139). I am not aware of any authoritative document from any world religion that states it so explicitly: *we are part of nature!* And therein lies our redemption and salvation.

We cannot evolve and realize a more authentic life as earthlings without a whole new immersion in the creation to which we belong. This is our deepest archetypal identity, our God-given gift of organic life. This is the coming-of-age, the spiritual homecoming, we have been pursuing amid the patriarchal distortions of recent millennia. Historically, in terms of our evolving story of some 7 million years, we have known this earthly symbiosis from time immemorial, long before the patriarchal emergence of the past few thousand years that has seriously disrupted our interdependence with the organic web of life.

Our true humanity belongs to the earth and to all that constitutes the cosmic web of life, and in this interconnected web there is no metaphysical difference between the human and divine. The two are intimately intertwined, as many of the great mystics have evidenced. The divine life force that animates and sustains the natural world is vastly more real than the supernatural imperial ruler above the sky that the patriarchs projected. Our natural homecoming is also our supernatural salvation. We were never a species in exile, and we were never intended to be. It is a remnant of our internalized oppression, a convoluted attempt to keep us subdued under patriarchal control.

In the Christian narrative, Jesus provides a template of what that archetypal human, natural identity looks like, and how we can best live it. In this part of the book I am attempting a fresh rehabilitation of that archetypal model. This is where coming-of-age becomes more transparent and empowering. Before going deeper, however, we still have to clear away some more clutter, this time the imperial baggage that has haunted all the major world religions.

6

The Postkingship Horizon

When Constantine gained his military victory under the sign of the Cross, the conflation of the Kingdom of God and the Empire of Caesar became an essential part of Christian history and theology.

—Wendy Farley

If civilization saves us from barbarism, what will save us from civilization?

—John D. Crossan

❄

Personal Reflection

Some years ago, I was asked to lead a day's reflection for a group of Anglican clergy in the United Kingdom, having agreed with the organizers to use this title: "Discipleship in the Kingdom of God Today." At the end of the day, one participant informed me that he came to the event largely out of curiosity—to see how I would manage to speak on the kingdom of God for a whole day, a topic that, he informed me, he found hard to speak about for more than fifteen minutes.

Reflecting on his remark, I began to realize that the same was true of myself in the early years of my priestly ministry. I have no recollection of the kingdom of God being emphasized or explained in any detail in my theological and scriptural studies. I do recall occasional mention of equating kingdom with Church, leaving me with the impression that it was the Church that really mattered, and that by serving the Church we were automatically being faithful to the kingdom of God.

Thanks to my missionary colleague, Adrian B. Smith (1996), whom I first met about ten years after ordination, I began to realize that the role of the Church is to be servant and herald of the kingdom of God, a conviction that was already in vogue in early Christian times but had eluded me in my theological formation. The first book I read on this topic was John Fuellenbach's classic presentation The Kingdom of God *(1994); this seminal work opened up for me an exploration into deeper Christian meaning that continues to the present.*

Only in the early years of the present century did I take to heart the words of the Sermon on the Mount: "Seek first *the kingdom of God" (Matt. 6:33, emphasis added). Such prioritizing is not merely about adjustments in the belief and practice of faith. More daunting still is the challenge of language and conceptualization. So much Christian rhetoric, even the language of Scripture itself, is based on the appropriation and affirmation of earthly kingship. God is a king, so Jesus must be one too. A great deal of Christian devotion, as practiced among the poor and oppressed, is based on a codependent plea for God's mercy, imploring the mighty, heavenly king for help and salvation.*

For myself, the single greatest conversion was the gradual awareness that we Christians have been hoodwinked for centuries, not just by church teaching but by Christian scholarship as well. We have been told so often to fear and respect God, the great king; be loyal and obedient, as royal servants should be; and humbly accept our passive, unworthy status. As I have delved deeper into the reality of the kingdom of God, and changed the language in that process, perhaps the single greatest challenge is the realization that Jesus brought a whole new reign of God in which we are all called to be adult codisciples, serving and earthing this new empowering dispensation. The implications are spelled out in the present chapter.

Jesus entered a world haunted by the embattled failure of patriarchal power. The kings had failed to deliver an empowering way of being; the prophets had produced a denouncing rhetoric, but failed to change the prevailing power systems; the apocalyptic forecast of God's imminent cataclysmic judgment brought a measure of reassurance that God was still in control, but failed to produce a breakthrough. A new imagination was desperately needed—and some rightly argue it is still needed—a strategy that would be visionary but also immensely practical. Jesus rose to the occasion, not with another panacea but with a transformative vision that could modify human and earthly reality in a substantial way.

Did Jesus succeed? Perhaps the more relevant question is, did humans allow him to succeed? In a previous work (O'Murchu 2005), I argue that it has taken us two thousand years to catch up with Jesus—and we are still trying to catch up. I sincerely believe we will get there eventually, but first we must unravel and discard the barriers we have put in the way throughout the past two thousand years, and at the forefront is our perverse addiction to patriarchal, kinglike power. That more than anything else has screwed up not merely the promised liberation of Christianity but the liberative, empowering praxis at the heart of all the great world religions.

Since the mid-twentieth century, Scripture scholars and theologians have been sorting through the inherited baggage and pointing us in a more promising and proactive direction. This is how Spanish theologian José Antonio Pagola (2009) states the challenge:

> The reign of God could only be proclaimed out of a close, direct contact with the people who most needed breathing space and liberation. The good news of God could not come from the splendid palace of Antipas in Tiberias, or from the sumptuous villas in Sepphoris, or from the wealthy neighborhood where the priestly elites lived in Jerusalem. The seeds of God's reign would only find fertile soil among the poor of Galilee. (98)

Scholars also detect in this new vision—described in the Gospels as the kingdom of God—an emerging phenomenon with few if any precedents in the Hebrew Scriptures or in the intertestamental literature (see Meier 1994, 289, 402; Pagola 2009, 100). We are encountering a novel construct, the fuller meaning of which requires a discerning analysis of archetypal depth, as offered throughout this chapter.

A Timely Breakthrough

The timing of this new breakthrough is a quandary that has engaged scholars for well over one hundred years. The Gospels speak of a future kingdom but also indicate that it is already happening in the here and now, what the scholars describe as *realized eschatology*. How to reconcile or combine those two time-dimensions is a challenge that scholars have never resolved. John P. Meier (1994) devotes a chapter to each position, with a clear preference for the future orientation, which fits well with his foundational conviction that Jesus is an end-of-the-age prophet marking the inbreaking of the eschatological fulfillment for which Israel had long yearned.

What is unclear is the shape of that new Israel. Is our earthly condition so transformed and renewed that it feels like a new, idyllic world where death will be no more and all creatures live harmoniously, as allegedly was the case before the "fall"? Or is it a heavenly transformed reality that has effectively left the material creation behind, as John P. Meier (1994) claims? "Jesus was not interested in and did not issue pronouncements about concrete social and political reforms, either for the world in general or for Israel in particular. He was not proclaiming the reform of the world; he was proclaiming the end of the world" (331).

To the best of my knowledge, most Scripture scholars disagree with Meier's interpretation, favoring instead a transformed creation in which the evolutionary imperative outlined in chapter 3 of this book could grow and flourish, and humans could enjoy and relish a world in which the meaningless pain and suffering of our time would be considerably reduced.

Considering which outcome Jesus had in mind becomes the critical question. At face value it is unclear from the Gospels. Statements like, "You will not have gone round the towns of Israel before the Son of Man come" (Matt. 10:23), cannot be taken literally (as many commentators suggest), although several fundamentalist Christians adopt this line—forever forecasting the imminent judgment of God and not seemingly put off by the fact that it never arrives. Here we encounter one of those delicate interpretative challenges of how far to move beyond a literal (historical) reading on the one hand, and a theological interpretation (eschatological fulfillment) on the other, and instead opt for a third possibility, which in the present work I describe as the *archetypal horizon*.

In archetypal terms, time is a continuum of past-present-future. We need all three dimensions to grasp the deeper meaning that transcends all our rational capabilities. And in evolutionary terms the future is what beckons us on in anticipation of that which is forever unfolding anew (see Haught 2017). Virtually all scholarly discourse, religious and secular, considers the past to be the most foundational of the three, and Darwinian evolution supports this view—but not the enlarged understanding of coevolution that marks our coming-of-age in the twenty-first century.

Ever since the seminal work of Albert Schweitzer, a large cohort of scholars have engaged the search for the historical Jesus. Some—probably the majority—have done so within the theological context of viewing Jesus as a prophetic, eschatological figure marking the end of an age, and inaugurating a new, transcendent realm, variously understood; scholars such as N. T. Wright and John P. Meier represent this perspective. Ever since the mid-twentieth century, there seems to be a substantial swing toward the evolutionary approach combining past-present-future (however, a present more informed by the future than by the past), perceived to be a call and commitment to make the world a better place not merely for humans but for all creatures. In this understanding of the kingdom of God, Jesus is viewed as the primary disciple of this new dispensation and all other humans are called to be codisciples in an evolving project that belongs to an open-ended future. John D. Crossan and other members of the Jesus Seminar are at the forefront in adopting this position.[1]

We may never discover what the historical Jesus had in mind in terms of the time-context for this new dispensation. What we do know is that it was a phenomenon of central importance for Jesus, and as I indicate later, a countercultural challenge not merely to the imperial culture of his day but indeed to royal dis-

---

[1] In passing we also need to note another position, adopted mainly by Catholics and fundamentalist Christians, for whom the church is the primary, and the only valid, articulation of the kingdom of God at work in the world. Many who adopt the position of Jesus as an eschatological prophet of the end time would view the church as the organism that keeps the vision of the kingdom alive until the end arrives. In the Catholic context, until about 1960, the kingdom of God was often equated with the Church, but increasingly since then, the kingdom is deemed to be greater than the Church, following a view adopted in early Christian times in which the church was described as the servant and herald of the kingdom (elaborated further by Fuellenbach 1994).

pensations of every time and age. This expansive horizon transcends the long-debated distinctions between a present and future kingdom of God. And we who represent the living Christ today—the body of Christ on earth now—need to err on the side of an expansive and empowering vision not merely for our own human future (salvation/redemption) but for that of all the other creatures who share the web of life with us. In all probability, that is what a contemporary Jesus would want us to do.

The Expansive Horizon

First, we need to acknowledge that this new vision is for everybody, rich and poor alike, with a more immediate benefit for those living in poverty and oppression. It is not just for Christians but for everybody, and one of the great scandals of history is that this new reign of God has often been lived out in far more authentic ways by non-Christians and nonbelievers than by Christians. More importantly for our time—the coming-of-age engaging us in this book—is the growing realization that this novel dispensation is not merely for humans but for all creatures inhabiting the web of universal life. The following quotations seem to embrace this enlarged horizon, although neither make it explicit:

- "Strictly speaking, Jesus did not bring God's Reign into the world, for it was already there. What Jesus did was to engage people in the manifestation of it, to enable them to know it is there, and to open their mind's eye to see it" (Song 1993, 162).
- "What Christian revelation reveals to us is nothing new, since such truths as it makes explicit must already be known to us implicitly in every moment of our existence" (Ogden 1986, 43).

Scholars have tended to interpret these statements too narrowly, pointing to the Hebrew Scriptures and particularly the covenantal vision as the reality that was already there. The quotations point us not merely to the inherited wisdom of the Hebrew Scriptures but to the revelation of God awakening *throughout the entire creation*. This new reign of God is not just about humans, nor their spiritual view of life outlined in one or another set of Scriptures. It embraces the whole context of our being and becoming, the grand archetypal arc of God's creation. In archetypal terms, therefore, we can assert in conjunction with nineteenth-century German Scripture scholar Ernst Troeltsch, "Jesus did not bring the kingdom of God; it is the kingdom of God that brought Jesus" (qtd. by Robert Hannaford in Hall 1996, 29).

American scholar Wes Howard-Brook (2011; 2016) provides a valued and informed overview of this enlarged horizon, tracing the foundational reign of God in our world to the story of creation as outlined in the opening chapter of Genesis. This same divine solidarity with all creation underpins the notion of the kingdom of God in the Christian gospel: "Jesus of Nazareth proclaimed the 'reign of God' in accordance with the pattern of the religion of creation, while denouncing the religion of empire as a demonic counterfeit" (Howard-Brook 2016, xiii). I suspect the biggest hurdle for truly understanding Jesus—even to this day—is the enlarged worldview out of which he operated. For Jesus it was all about encountering God in the open space and universality of creation, and not merely in the closed precincts of temple, synagogue, church, or mosque. His vision was neither anti- nor postreligion. It was of an entirely different global ambience.

Theologian Elizabeth Johnson concurs with the view that the reign of God is rooted in the Hebrew Bible. However, she interprets this Hebrew source within an expansive horizon, advocating a global, transpersonal vision:

> For this was the kingdom of the redeeming, saving God of Israel. Slaves would be freed, exiles returned home; springs would flow in the desert, abundance mark the fields; justice would be established and mercy reign. In a word, the

symbol refers to the state of the world when the will of
God is finally and fully honored: compassion and kindness
will abound, joy and peace will break out, and all creation will flourish. Jesus's use of this particular symbol was
inherently subversive. His announcement turned the usual
operations of the kingdoms of this world on their heads.
God's way of ruling was the opposite of the empire's Caesar. (2018, 75)

So, God's ever-new reign in its primordial archetypal meaning
refers to the whole cosmic creation. *This is God's primary revelation to us.* This is where we experience the creative empowerment of God primarily at work, and since ours is an evolutionary
creation forever unfolding in grandeur and complexity, then that
revelation never ceases and is forever new. Particularly perplexing
for humans is that creation's evolutionary story is characterized by
breakdown and breakthrough (see chapter 3 above). It is infused
by paradox manifested in the recurring cycle of birth-death-
rebirth. It is an imperfect creation, always awaiting a greater sense
of completion, which is never a finished product. This understanding conflicts with our imperialistic understanding of God as an
all-knowing and all-powerful creator.

But where did we get this understanding of God? Basically
from the patriarchal consciousness that unfolded in the wake
of the agricultural revolution some eight thousand to ten thousand years ago. In the case of the conventional Christian story,
we inherited the notion of an imperial God from classical Greek
philosophy and its progeny, Scholasticism. It is alien to the understanding of God we have experienced throughout the long eons
of our human evolution.

So, the new reign of God is *cosmic* in its universal outreach,
but it is also transpersonal in its archetypal significance. It is not
merely a salvific remedy for the power-hungry creatures who
evolved on earth in the wake of the agricultural revolution. God
has been reigning in the human spirit ever since we began to

evolve as a human species, some *7 million years ago* in terms of our protohuman status; or 3.5 million years ago in our emerging identity as *Homo* (fully human; see more in O'Murchu 2008). How exactly we understood God—and God's reign in creation—throughout this long time span is something we can glean—at least partially—from indigenous faith traditions that we are rediscovering today. Foremost among these is belief in the Great Spirit, a belief system known to several indigenous groups throughout the contemporary world and outlined in great detail in this book's final chapter.

In incarnational terms, therefore, God's embodied presence in our world belongs first and foremost to the universal, cosmic creation. Thereafter we discern that same reign of God in every evolutionary, embodied development, including that of our own species. How the conventional Christian understanding of incarnation in the person of Jesus can be integrated with the enlarged horizons I am describing is a task theologians have not yet undertaken. One gets the impression that many are not even aware of the urgency of such an undertaking.

Historical Background

In the previous chapter I highlighted some of the historical precedents we need to keep in mind in the evolution of the patriarchally influenced religions we know today. I need to add some further cultural insight indicating how we lost archetypal spiritual wisdom in the sellout to imperial consciousness.

The growing body of archaeological evidence suggests that for some six thousand years the Canaanites were a horticultural/agricultural people, with substantial evidence also for creative handiwork with pottery and later with metal. Their lifestyle and values for most of this time suggest an egalitarian tribal existence.[2] But with continuous incursions from surrounding powers,

---

[2] Although concerned primarily with the social and economic con-

especially from the Philistines, the Canaanites thought they could better resist these invaders if they also adopted a monarchy, the protection of a ruling king on par with all the other nations. Wes Howard-Brook (2011, 199–211) provides a valuable overview of this transitional period and concludes that the Israel of the Hebrew Bible comes into existence only with the Davidic monarchy in the tenth century BCE (202).

From this point on, kingship becomes an integral dimension of Israel's turbulent history, characterized by a great deal of violence and warfare, with some disturbing portrayals of God as a violent, vindictive deity, supporting brutality and imperial domination. For those who tried to remain faithful to the covenant, a more peaceful and egalitarian coexistence prevailed. Thus, for the people of Israel, the God that led them out of captivity in Egypt was viewed as a liberator and shepherd, bestowing on the people a quality of care and protection like that of a loving father. According to Spanish theologian José Antonio Pagola (2009), this God was not compared to a king. Nonetheless, the imperial divine system progressively took over and became the basis for political and religious values alike.

Over time the people lost faith in kingly governance. "Despite the warnings of the prophets," writes Pagola (2009), "Israel had become a disaster because of the kings' favoritism towards the powerful, the exploitation of the poor by the wealthy, and every other kind of abuse. The consequences of all this was their exile in Babylonia" (101). While generating a sense of hope, the prophetic voice failed to change the unjust plight of the people. At the beginning of the second century BCE, a new literary genre came to the fore. Known as *apocalyptic literature*, the book of Daniel is one of its better-known texts, and according to James Carroll (2014), it heavily influenced all the Gospel writers. These writings are popularly understood as declaring a final intervention by God,

---

ditions at the time of Jesus, Fiensy (2014) provides several insights into this ancient egalitarian way of life.

who would destroy the present corrupt world and replace it with a new heaven and a new earth—and the God who would make that possible would himself be a king, but in a manner superior to all forms of earthly kingship.[3]

This brief overview can scarcely do justice to a rather complex historical and cultural situation. However, it does indicate how kingship came to be regarded as God's favorite mode of governance. What later came to be known as the divine right of kings was not a feature only of ancient Israel but was evidenced in several contemporaneous cultures, including in China, India, Mesopotamia, Babylon, and Egypt. By the time Jesus comes on the scene there was an unquestioned conviction that God's authentic liberator would come from a royal line. In the time of Jesus, King David was the one who headed the lineage.

An Upside-Down Kingdom

What did Jesus do with this inherited, divinely validated kingship? The short answer is: nothing. He seems to have disassociated himself completely from it and denounced it whenever an opportunity arose. Not so the evangelists, however, who were strongly indoctrinated in the notion that God's great liberators would be of a royal line, which they trace back to King David (in the case of Matthew), to Abraham (in the case of Luke), and to God the original king (in the case of John). Even if the royal lines had some historical veracity—and as far as I know, they don't—Jesus himself would not have attributed any significance to them. To the core of his being, Jesus was anti-imperialistic.

This creates a serious problem for the language of the New Testament. The Greek *He Basileia tou Theou* translates in Eng-

---

[3] A number of contemporary Scripture scholars, notably John P. Meier, N. T. Wright, and Richard Horsley, claim that the apocalyptic vision should be understood as a transformation of this earthly realm, beginning with the historical transformation of Israel itself, an outcome sometimes described as eschatological.

lish as *the kingdom of God*. But if Jesus does not belong to royal patronage, and he contested it to its core, then how can *we* be justified in using such language? The fact that the Gospel writers, whom we deem to be divinely inspired, used such language is no longer an argument that commands credibility. Whatever the level of their inspiration, the four evangelists were clearly influenced by the prevailing culture of their day and its imperial baggage.

What then can we do with the inappropriate language? I allude briefly to this dilemma in previous works (O'Murchu 2011; 2014a; 2017), and in the end, I have chosen to run with a renaming that might resemble the original Aramaic (cf. John Dominic Crossan 1991, 421–22), namely, the *companionship of empowerment*.[4] Although initially this term sounds awkward to a lot of people, I suspect it comes close to what was really important for the historical Jesus—and also opens up possibilities for illuminating the archetypal significance of his life and ministry. *Empowerment* transcends the addiction to patriarchal power, suggesting that every other (persons and inorganic) can participate in shared power.

Of the term's two key words, *companionship* is the more revolutionary. It denotes mutuality and community, but with a subtle and all-important undertow. Of course, empowerment could also be activated by a benign king. My contention, however, is that Jesus would not be interested in any kind of king, benign or otherwise; he wanted an end to all forms of kingship, to be replaced by a whole new, empowering dynamic based on mutual participation and interdependence (similar to the *communal obedience* described in chapter 2 above). He wanted every pyramid replaced with a circle, and every hierarchy yielding pride of place to the holarchical structure evidenced throughout creation.[5]

---

[4] More recently, Crossan (2010) seems to favor another renaming: the Household of God, with household (Greek: *oikos*) understood in cosmic/planetary terms as well as in its local usage for house and home.

[5] Biologists frequently reference nested hierarchies that they detect throughout creation. I suspect that such observations arise from their

The companionship of empowerment makes a double shift: from power-over to power-with, and from unilateral domination to communal collaboration (more in Crossan 2010). It marks a seismic shift from exclusivity to radical inclusiveness. As in our time, so also in the time of Jesus, the royal dispensation was heavily couched in elitism and exclusion. Royal patronage was often reserved for specific families, and within the exercise of kingly power, only the privileged few obtained close access. The king's palace was heavily fortified, and admission was only allowed to a selected elite. Opulence and glory befitted royal accolade, far in excess of what ordinary people could ever hope to experience. Between the king and the people stood a vast chasm. It seems that the historical Jesus declared an end to such imperial exclusion, a breakthrough captivated by Wendy Farley (2011) in these words: "In this empire [kingdom of God] neither victims nor perpetrators find the door slammed in their faces. . . . If we accept its healing, we are asked to accept that everyone else in the entire world is a citizen of this kingdom" (204).

In the companionship of empowerment, one of the ground rules seems to be that nobody is out, and therefore everybody is considered to be included. Moreover, no longer are power and privilege reserved to the select few. The pyramid has been transformed into a circle. Animation is activated from the center outward in an embrace that excludes no one. The "privileges" of this new dispensation belong primarily to those who have never known anything but exclusion: the poor, the marginalized, the despised, the disenfranchised. It has aptly been described as an upside-down kingdom (Kraybill 1990).

John Shelby Spong (2016) claims that Paul's extensive use of the notion of *righteousness*, which frequently appears in the letter to the Romans, may be considered an equivalent to the

---

academic conditioning, and thus to see what they expect to see—a kind of self-fulfilling prophesy. For the holarchical understanding of creation, see Currivan (2017).

Gospels' notion of the kingdom of God, with the central focus on right relating, in the name of love, justice, liberation, and empowerment:

> The kingdom of God comes when we are empowered to live fully, to love wastefully and to be all that we are capable of being. It means that the work of the kingdom of God is the work of enhancing human wholeness. . . . It means that the work of the kingdom of God is done when the eyes of the blind are opened to see reality undistorted by religious propaganda and the ears of the deaf are opened to listen to truth even when it threatens our religious security. It means that the limbs of the twisted, the crippled and the broken will be able to leap with joy as new humanity breaks in upon us without the distortions of our tribal past. It means that the voices of those once muted by fear can sing as they watch all the life-denying prejudices that separate human beings into destructive camps fade away and die. That will be the time when the kingdom of God becomes visible, and that will be when God's righteousness—for which, without always knowing it, human beings have both hungered and thirsted—will finally be revealed. (140)

Archetypal Identity in the New Companionship

It seems that Jesus began his public ministry as a disciple of John the Baptist. Why he opted out—and what he opted into—is not clear, but a shift from a more ascetical strategy for reform to one postulated on healing and commensality seems highly significant. Remember that remarkable passage: "For John came neither eating not drinking, and they say, 'He has a demon!' The Son of Man came eating and drinking, and they say, 'Look at this glutton and drunkard, a friend of tax collectors and of sinners!' But wisdom is vindicated by her actions" Matt. 11:18).

In Luke 7 and Matthew 11 the disciples of John seek clarity from Jesus on what he is about exactly. Why John sent them to ask the question is unclear. Was John himself in his execution cell having doubts, or was he concerned more for the future welfare of his followers? It is also impossible to know how they heard and interpreted the answer Jesus gave them: "Go and tell John what you have seen and heard; the blind receive their sight, the lame walk, lepers are cleaned, and the deaf hear, the dead are raised up, the poor have good news preached to them. And blessed is the one who takes no offense at me" (Lk. 7:22–23). These words are generally interpreted as the messianic promise outlined in Isaiah 35 and 42, indicating that Jesus indeed is the expected Messiah, thus reassuring John and his disciples in the face of their fears and doubts. We are not told how John felt about this response.

Taken at its face value, the text evokes a quality of rational response. But can we be sure that rationality is the appropriate vein in which to read either the question from John, or more particularly, the response from Jesus? Are we not dealing with an archetypal horizon here, with substantial implications for biblical exegesis and the living out of our Christian faith today? The question posed by John's disciples can also be viewed as a question of identity. Effectively, the disciples are asking, who exactly are you? Throughout the Gospels, Jesus engages questions of identity with the rhetoric of parable rather than rational speech. Why not adopt the same strategy here?

A rational answer to the question would ensue with Jesus pointing the finger to himself and, in loyalty to Aristotelian expectation, proceeding to describe himself as the Messiah or adopting a set of characteristics to illuminate his God-given messianic mission. But in addressing John's disciples, Jesus points the finger away from himself.[6] As Robert Funk (1996) suggested many years

---

[6] Noteworthy is the observation of John P. Meier (1994): "Jesus did not usually put himself explicitly at the center of his preaching. Rather, the kingdom of God, not Jesus as the proclaimer of the king-

ago, the direction of the pointing finger may be highly sugges-
tive and rich in symbolic meaning. Jesus points the finger *away*
from himself and not toward himself. But what does he point it
toward?

> Jesus pointed to something he called God's domain, some-
> thing he did not create, something he did not control. I
> want to discover what Jesus saw, or heard, or sensed that
> was so enchanting, so mesmerizing, so challenging that it
> held Jesus in its spell. And I do not want to be misled by
> what the followers did: instead of looking to see what he
> saw, the devoted disciples tended to stare at the pointing
> finger. Jesus himself should not be, must not be, the object
> of faith. That would be to repeat the idolatry of the first
> believers. (Funk 1996)

"The blind see, the deaf hear. . . ." Is this not the new reign of
God taking shape? Is Jesus not pointing his finger directly at the
companionship of empowerment, my proposed renaming of the
kingdom of God? So, what is he actually saying to the disciples of
John? *"Stop looking at me, the individual savior, and look instead
toward my relational matrix, the web of my mission, from which
I, the individual Jesus—and you, too—receive personal identity
and discipleship for mission."* Is Jesus confronting John's disciples
with a whole new sense of what it means to be a person: *relational, inclusive,* and *empowering*? Is he not challenging the disciples to cease gaping at some isolated divine hero (influenced by
Greek philosophy), and look instead at the empowering divine
presence in their midst embodied in the communal web of creation
itself? In archetypal terms, we are dealing with the transpersonal

---

dom, was the main object of Jesus's preaching. The kingdom was the
reality he sought to communicate, however partially or proleptically,
by activities such as exorcism and table fellowship with sinners" (421;
see also 438, 453).

rather than the personal, understood—as it is conventionally named today—in reductionistic Aristotelian anthropology.

Toward a Relational Anthropology

Throughout the modern world, the Aristotelian definition of the human person dictates our social constructions of reality in politics, economics, education, science, and religion. There are meager residues of an alternative anthropology in some of our tribal cultures and among First Nations peoples. In Africa, one occasionally still hears allusions to the notion of *Ubuntu*: "I am because we are." Contemporary anthropology and psychology (see Boeve et al. 2014) occasionally seek to reinstate this subverted view of the human with this cryptic assertion: *I am at all times the sum of my relationships, and this is what gives me identity.* Human identity is not merely a once-off accomplishment but rather a lifelong process, unfolding over time and involving a complex range of influences: cosmic, planetary, organic, human, and spiritual. David G. Kirchhoffer offers the following useful résumé:

> Possibly the primary challenge to theological anthropology is that twenty-first-century theology will not be defined by who or what the human person is (the classical questions of a substance metaphysics), but by *where* in the world the person is. . . . Whereas the tradition has usually talked about the person being IN the world, the great realization of the latter half of the twentieth century may indeed be that we ARE the world. We are so fundamentally bound up in an infinite network of relationships that to even conceive of some sort of objective self or human essence verges on the absurd. (See Boeve et al. 2014, 185.)

And let's add the Christian challenge, captivated succinctly by Walter Wink (2002): "Incarnation is a task for us all to accomplish and not just some divine attribute of the historical Jesus" (157).

Regarding the new relational paradigm, Albert Einstein captivated quite beautifully what is at stake in a remarkable letter written to a friend, grieving the loss of a loved one:

> A human being is a part of the whole called by us universe, a part limited in time and space. He experiences himself, his thoughts and feelings as something separated from the rest, a kind of optical delusion of his consciousness. This delusion is a kind of prison for us, restricting us to our personal desires and to affection for a few persons nearest to us. Our task must be to free ourselves from this prison by widening our circle of compassion to embrace all living creatures and the whole of nature in its beauty. (qtd. in Calaprice 2005, 206)

Israeli/French psychoanalyst Bracha Ettinger (2006) also lends voice to reclaiming an alternative anthropology, which situates the capacity for relationship as foundational to human flourishing, from the earliest stages of development in the mother's womb. That matrixial bond is the primal foundation that programs each human life for interconnection, interdependence, and cooperation, and not for the separate individualism (substance) propounded by Aristotle—and so cherished by the patriarchal male, whose view of life is often tainted by the allure of separation, domination, and competition, the key characteristics of what Lyons (2015) calls the *phallic culture.*

Modern brain science is also moving in this same direction. Inspired by the Connectome project, we witness today a rapidly growing body of brain research pointing us away from the previous tendency to identify different parts of the brain and their influence on different aspects of human behavior, and toward the brain as a complex, interactive neural system—indicating, among other things, that our brains are programmed for interconnection and relationality. (For a good outlook on this pioneering work, see Seung 2012.)

According to this relational understanding, none of us can grow into what the Christian gospel (Jn. 10:10) calls the fullness of life, without being embedded in and sustained by a relational interconnectedness that spans the entire web of creation. There is no such thing as a lone individual. It is a distorted, patriarchal fantasy that alienates and undermines our true nature. All of us are programmed for relationship, and it is through our relational interdependence that we fulfill our deepest aspirations and contribute creatively to making the world a better place for all.

Empire or Creation?

American scholar Wes Howard-Brook (2011; 2016) provides a clear and compelling argument that God's intended reign in our world belongs first and foremost to the universal creation (as intimated in the poetic rendition in the opening verses of Genesis), and has been usurped and desecrated by the pursuit of human empire-building. Every major world religion is contaminated by the lure of imperial kingship, a by-product of the agricultural revolution. In the case of the Judeo-Christian religion it is an undeniable feature of the Hebrew Scriptures, with some disturbing patriarchal projections culminating in a ruling deity that seems quite violent and even barbaric at times.

Catholic scholar John P. Meier (1994) notes that while references to the kingship of God frequently occur in the Hebrew Scriptures and in the intertestamental literature, the phrase "kingdom of God" rarely occurs there, and when it does, it lacks that more decisive meaning that Jesus embraced, as evidenced in the Gospels. Meier also notes the tension between the kingdom as already present (realized eschatology) and its future realization—as God's coming anew to rule over Israel and the world at the end time—which, as noted earlier, he considers to be the primary significance of the kingdom of God.

Since the archetypal perspective tends to transcend dualistic splitting, the notions of the kingdom unfolding in the here and now and yet awaiting a future fulfillment should be seen as complementary rather than in opposition to each other. Today, we also hold the evolutionary viewpoint very much to the fore, and in evolutionary terms each present reality is an open-ended, not a closed, system; what is happening in the present is always informed not merely from the past but also by what John Haught (2015) calls the *lure of the future*. The lure can be understood to function like a strange attractor, energized by the creative Spirit of God, and not by a divine, imperial ruler from on high (more on the creative Spirit in chapter 10).

Whereas conventional Christian faith has tended to emphasize salvation in a life beyond the present, depicting the here and now as fundamentally flawed by original sin and its consequences, prioritizing the kingdom of God (as the companionship of empowerment) shifts the focus significantly in the direction of God's creation. The companionship of empowerment is not a prescriptive program to obtain salvation in a heaven hereafter. Rather it is about bringing about heaven on earth, collaborating with God—as Jesus did in an eminent way—to support and advance the evolutionary complexity within which creation is forever unfolding. John Dominic Crossan (2010) articulates the challenge with typical forthright clarity: *While we are waiting for God's intervention, God is actually waiting for our collaboration.*

Therefore fidelity to the kingdom, or serving the new companionship, has very little meaning for salvation and redemption as traditionally understood. The primary companionship into which every human is born as an earthling is the cosmic/planetary web of life. Our birthing into this reality is activated by the erotic fertility of the Great Spirit (more in chapter 10), and we in turn are missioned to be co-birthers (that is, cocreators) with our creative God in the empowering process, which is itself the evolutionary imperative that animates and sustains all life. Our personal and interpersonal "salvation" largely depends on our response to this lure of evolutionary transformation.

The new companionship of the Christian gospel—at the archetypal level—is never about human beings exclusively. We are invited to reclaim our integral place within the great cosmic and planetary web of life, and to serve the empowering mission of our God within that creative context. As I indicate in the next chapter, this is what many of the parables are elucidating—viewed from an archetypal perspective. We are not—and were never meant to be—violent, imperial exploiters of earth's resources. We are servants to an empowering vision that seeks out and promotes the flourishing of all sentient beings. Such is the horizon for our coming-of-age as a Christian people today.

To many readers this may sound excessively idealistic, even to the point of being wildly utopian. I stand accused of ignoring the sheer evil that grips our world today, the gross exploitation and ravaging of the fragile earth, the indisputable violence of original sin. Original sin has often been used as a smokescreen to distract us from the pernicious exploitation of imperial and patriarchal power, the root cause of so much of the world's evil. Even some of the great freaks of nature—earthquakes, tornadoes, and so on—are taking on added frequency and intensity because of misguided human interference.

Already in chapter 3, I alluded to the great paradox that characterizes all creation, named as the great paradox of creation-cum-destruction or the recurring cycle of birth-death-rebirth. This paradox underpins all suffering in our world, human and nonorganic alike. And most of the meaningless suffering that humans cause arises from our ignorance of, and inability to befriend, this foundational paradox. Jesus did not avoid this paradox, nor did he try to get rid of it, which would mean the end of all creation. Rather he entered deeply into it—in his life, death, and resurrection—and thus showed Christians how we also can engage the paradox more authentically. In this way, we begin to see that the new, empowering companionship requires humans to take a more direct responsibility for our own empowerment and that of our fellow beings. If we feel totally powerless, as patriarchal cultures often demand, then we cannot be disciples of the companionship of empowerment.

Some Concluding Observations

Discipleship of this new reign of God, as empowering companions, is a process that knows no closure. It is as open-ended and vast as creation itself and as intimate as the subatomic quarks that constitute all created reality. At the human level, Richard Rohr, Franciscan friar and spiritual guide, captivates something of this empowering universality when he writes (2009), "The Kingdom of God is the naked now—the world without human kingdoms, ethnic communities, national boundaries, or social identifications. That is about as subversive and universalist as you can get. But don't think about it too much; it will surely change your politics and your pocketbook" (101). This quotation also throws down the gauntlet for disciples' coming-of-age in the evolutionary maturity of our Christian faith.

Taking up the challenge to grow into such maturity knows no favorites or beneficiaries of special choice. There are no chosen people, precisely because all are chosen. We are all loved unconditionally, and that is our starting point. Some of us might be brilliant: others of us might be quite ordinary, whose daily lot may seem humdrum and uneventful. But we are each unique and special. The challenge is that our individual growth into deeper life (coming-of-age) cannot be achieved on our own, nor can it be delivered merely by allegiance to those who claim to know better.

Our convivial, empowering relationships make more real on earth the new companionship—the relational matrix—and constitute the heart and soul of Christian living. The flourishing of each is inescapably interconnected with the flourishing of all, and that capacity for mutual empowerment is what redemption and salvation mean in our evolutionary world.

Except for one big catch! As a species, we cannot do it on our own. In the grand scheme of things, let us never forget that we are earthlings, creatures born out of the earth and accountable to the entire cosmic creation. For us to flourish, everything must flourish, even in a world endowed with the paradox of creation-cum-destruction. The ability to hold that enlarged reality in our hearts and to integrate it into our daily lives—as individuals and communities—enables and empowers a truly graced coming-of-age. The intricate and intriguing nature of that challenge becomes much more transparent in the Gospels' parables, whose meaning we explore next.

7

The Subversive Horizon of Parable Narrative

Theology, with its inflated Western blocks of abstraction, has lost the economy of parable. . . . So we are learning again to speak God's Sophia in a mystery. . . . In a parable, the sense of resolve does not solve but deepens the mystery.

—Catherine Keller

When we interpret a parable, the goal should not be to "explain it" in clearer language than Jesus used, but to reawaken the experience it provoked when Jesus first told it.

—José Antonio Pagola

The disciples noticed that Jesus frequently invoked the notion of the companionship of empowerment. Whether they would have heard the words nuanced in the original Aramaic or with the Greek imperial intent is something we will probably never know for sure. However, it is clear from the Gospels that the disciples questioned Jesus on the meaning of this new vision.

They sought clarity, probably a rational answer, maybe even a nice, neat definition.

And what were they given? A story! "The companionship of empowerment may be compared to . . . : a man sowing seed in the field, a woman working leaven into the dough, workers in the vineyard, guests at a wedding feast."[1] All these images are familiar—in fact, too familiar for conceptual comfort then, or for doctrinal clarity in our time. These stories in gospel lore are known as the *parables*.

Aptly, the parables can be described as *queer stories*. In colloquial English, "queer" is a derogatory term, designating odd or unusual, and in homophobic culture, a derisory term for gay or lesbian persons. Fortunately, being creatures of imagination, humans can rescue even the most sordid linguistic devices and put them at the service of more noble aspirations. In recent years, "queering" has become almost a science in its own right. We read about "queering politics," "queering religion," and some Christian theologians, like Marcella Althaus-Reid (2003), talk about "queering" God and Christ.

Queer theory, whose origins are often traced to the French philosopher Michel Foucault, is now widely regarded as a field of serious academic research (see Sullivan 2003). Although initially focused on dethroning the cultural monopoly of heterosexism, it is now used as a cultural critique against every effort at imposing a straitjacket or monolithic understanding, whether in the sexual, social, or cultural realms. Using irony, ridicule,

---

[1] Using the parables in direct reference to the kingdom of God is very much a Matthean device. Zimmermann (2015, 63n30, 93–94) claims that only thirteen parables deal directly with the kingdom. Luke never makes a direct comparison, despite the fact that several of the more memorable parables we have inherited describe much more vividly the alternative understanding of the kingdom of God as the companionship of empowerment. Nonetheless, several contemporary scholars would endorse this concluding observation of James G. D. Dunn (2003): "Jesus was evidently remembered as using parables to illustrate or illumine what he had in mind when he spoke of the kingdom" (385).

parody, and the elasticity of language itself, queer theory transgresses culturally approved rationality, exposing inconsistencies and incongruities, particularly around the abusive use of power. Instead, it proffers more open-ended, fluid paradigms invoking the extensive use of imagination, intuition, and playfulness. In many ways it prepares the ground for a deeper appreciation of archetypal meaning.

This is precisely what we encounter in the parables of the Gospels. Jesus is into queering on a big scale—and we need to remember, he is doing so at the service of a new countercultural vision, renamed in the last chapter as the companionship of empowerment. Furthermore, I suggest that is through the engagement with parable-narrative that Jesus invites and challenges people into an elevated level of adult discernment characteristic of the coming-of-age outlined in the present work.

Disturbing Countercultural Stories

The parables mark a paradigm shift of rare ingenuity. They require extensive imagination, intuition, and a quality of prophetic wisdom that is truly unique. They plunge the hearer into the subliminal depths of archetypal meaning. And a coming-of-age is certainly required to wrestle with their subversive, transgressive challenges. The following are statements from just three contemporary Scripture scholars:

> Just at the point in the story line when the reader is lured into its internal logic, [the parable] takes an unexpected and unforeseen twist, and one is left wondering what the point really was. As a pedagogic device, this unusual twist in the story line engages the hearer's imagination to rethink their own presuppositions and re-evaluate their notions on what the "Kingdom of God" might really be like. (Freyne 2014, 161)

While certainly communicating Jesus's prophetic message,
the parables have at the same time a teasing indeterminacy,
an openness to more than one meaning or application that
makes them especially suited to draw people (learned and
unlearned alike) into dialogue, challenging their presup-
positions and opening up new horizons that the audience
must ponder without the comfort of pat answers supplied
by the teacher. (Meier 2016, 34)

The parable should disturb. If we hear it and are not disturbed, there is something seriously amiss with our moral
compass. It would be better if we perhaps started by seeing
the parable not as about heaven or hell or final judgment,
but about kings, politics, violence, and the absence of justice. If we do, we might be getting closer to Jesus. (Levine
2014, 282)

A vast literature exists on the parables; for a well-informed
overview, see Ruben Zimmermann (2015), and for a more scholarly rendition, see Klyne Snodgrass (2008). While scholars still
debate precise meaning and methods of interpretation, there is
widespread agreement on the parables' original provocative
nature. American scholar John P. Meier (2016) devotes a substantial tome to the Gospel parables, marked by a comprehensive
overview of study and research on them.[2] Meier (2016) strongly

---

[2] At the end of this thoroughly scholarly enterprise, Meier concludes that only four of all the parables recorded in the Gospels can
be considered as reliable evidence for the historical Jesus. These are the
Mustard Seed (Mk. 4:30–32), the Evil Tenants of the Vineyard (Mk.
12:1–11), the Great Supper (Matt. 22:2–14), and the Talents (Matt.
25:14–30). Many of the most memorable parables in Christian lore
are from Luke's Gospel, which Meier considers to be Lukan inven-
tions that cannot be traced back to the historical Jesus. Clearly his controversial conclusions are determined by his selected criteria, primary
among which is his Christological view that Jesus is an end-of-the-age
eschatological prophet, fulfilling the Old Testament promise of a new

emphasizes a connection with the Hebrew Scriptures, suggesting that Jesus, the parable narrator, belongs to the Old Testament prophetic tradition, and that Jesus's use of the parables should be viewed primarily as a continuation of the prophetic call:

> Jesus seems in his parable telling to have reached back quite consciously to the Former and Latter Prophets of the Jewish Scriptures instead of simply reflecting the more recent apocalyptic or sapiential literature of Israel. . . . The historical Jesus presented himself to his fellow 1st-century Palestinian Jews first and foremost as the Elijah-like prophet of the end time. . . . We need not be surprised that many of Jesus's parables carry an eschatological tone, though the parable genre was flexible enough to serve more than one aspect of Jesus's mission and message. (40–41)

Serving more than one aspect is precisely the purpose of this book, since the archetypal depth I am seeking to explore and reclaim requires this eclectic breadth of discernment. Even Meier himself (2016, 38) concedes that the Hebrew notion of *mashal* (parable) carries a more specified application than we find in the prophetic narratives. For José Pagola (2009), this more specified application is the new reign of God:

> Only Jesus told parables about the "reign of God." The teachers of the law used several kinds of *mashal* in their

---

Israel, which God will bring about at the end of time, by divine initiative and not by human enterprise. However, there are a range of alternative scholarly views, which I outline to support the wider analysis that considers the parables to be (1) primary data for a deeper, more engaging understanding of the kingdom of God, and particularly understood as the companionship of empowerment; and (2) foundational narratives to illuminate the archetypal perspective being explored in the present work. Whether one agrees or disagrees with Meier's conclusions, volume 5 of his reputed *A Marginal Jew* (2016) is an invaluable resource for study of the parables.

teaching, some of them similar in form and content to Jesus's parables, but for very different purposes. In general, the rabbis began with a biblical text that they wanted to explain to their disciples, and used a parable to expound the correct interpretation of the law. Therein lies the fundamental difference: the rabbis were seeing things from a legal perspective while Jesus is revisioning reality from the perspective of the reign of God that was already irrupting in Israel. (125)

For the people of Israel, the parables evoke a new threshold for coming-of-age. The distant God whom they could never call by name, who spoke from the pillar of a cloud or a burning bush, now communicates through the communal interaction of ordinary people. It is a kind of wake-up call from passive dependency to proactive collaboration, a new level of adult maturity of faith, with substantial implications for life then and now. Rarely have commentaries even named this central feature of the parables.[3] The following are some of the key features I wish to highlight:

- Parables as told by Jesus have a distinctive subversive flavor with few precedents in ancient Hebrew literature. These are stories that challenge and disturb several sanctioned cultural and moral norms.
- Parables stretch conventional wisdom to the breaking point—and beyond.
- Parables leave the hearer with dislocated feelings and a need for major conceptual adjustments.

---

[3] Commentators as well as preachers and teachers tend to emphasize the ordinariness and simplicity of the parable narratives, even making them accessible to children. Children can certainly grasp the basic content: the story of the Good Samaritan is memorable and easy to recall. But to discern the deeper, complex, and subversive meaning of the parable requires a great deal of adult intellect and a well-developed capacity for adult discernment.

- Parables resolve nothing; rather they open up reality into a vast range of fresh, new possibilities.
- All the parables require inclusiveness of previously excluded dimensions of life.
- The parables break through the dualistic split between the sacred and the secular.

Remarkably, few commentators highlight the radical departure from the cultural expectation of the day, namely, that responsible males (particularly) strive to employ the rational and reasonable rhetoric of the prevailing Greek culture. Jesus openly—and perhaps consciously—flies in the face of this expectation. Second, few commentators truly honor the subversive tenor of these stories, William Herzog (1994) being one of the notable exceptions. And third, as already indicated, the adult dimension of such story engagement is rarely acknowledged.

Catechists try to simplify parables to make them more accessible to children (preachers tend to do the same thing), when Jesus actually used such stories to engage adult followers in adult-based discipleship in the service of an adult God. *The call to mature adulthood is deeply inscribed into the parabolic landscape.* To honor their subversive intent, along with their adult challenges, the following elements of parables need more discerning attention:

- The Gospel writers themselves seem to have departed significantly from the original purpose of the parables as Jesus told them.
- The Gospel writers—or other editors—tend to spiritualize and moralize the original stories, undermining their foundational political, economic, and spiritual counterculture.
- The tendency to allegorize the parables—that is, make ethical or spiritual comparisons based on them—frequently undermines and distorts the liberating empowerment of the original story.

- Interpretations that equate Jesus (or God) with the leading character (the king, the landlord) not only distract from the foundational message but mark a serious departure from the nonimperial vision of the new reign of God.
- Colonial mimicry—depicting God or Jesus as an imperial figure—features in many of the parables. This is more likely to be an editorial gloss rather than behavior that the historical Jesus would have adopted.
- Many parables adopt dualistic splitting (sheep versus goats; wise versus foolish virgins), a literary and cultural tactic of the time that the Hebrew Jesus is unlikely to have used.

Many of these distortions can be seen in the parable of the Workers in the Vineyard (Matt. 20:1–16), in which the landlord is frequently depicted as God, exemplifying a sense of justice and generosity that defies the normative practice of paying people in accordance with the service they have rendered. When one better understands the exploitative employment practices of the time, and the precarious plight of the expendables (see Herzog 1994; Horsley 2008), then we expose the blatant exploitation and economic oppression embodied in this narrative. In the name of the companionship of empowerment, another interpretation is needed, one more likely to be congruent with the historical Jesus as champion of the poor and oppressed. While the story at its face value can be heard in rhetorical prose, the truth of the parable is much more subtle and subversive. Poetry can immerse us more viscerally in the desire for justice and liberation, in all probability the virtues being evoked in the original telling of this parable:

The Generous Extortionist

The money he promised was not very much,
But at least 't would keep hunger at bay.
Nor did I expect we would still be at work

Right through to the end of the day.
Nor did any foresee the trick he would play
Exploiting our meager resource.

CHORUS:
"I'll do what I like with what is my own,
My generous spirit you treat with such scorn.
Take what is yours and go!"

Because we complained, we're often denounced
As selfish and greedy beside.
To question the power of a system in place
Yourself you set up to deride.
To destabilize the values supreme
And scorn the rhetoric so cruel:

CHORUS

Most sickening of all is the rhetoric's twist,
Depicting a generous crook.
We saw through the bullshit he sought to exploit
Whatever our ultimate luck.
And we tried to maintain a dignified stance
As he ranted imperial spake:

CHORUS

Despite all our setbacks and daily despair,
The Gospel still honors our plight.
And our yearning for justice will one day outwit
The ravage who seeks to exploit
Exposing corruption we must never cease,
The truth for our lives we will risk.

CHORUS

Although we're the victims who lost once again
And some feel embittered to rue.
Our hunger for justice is strongly enforced
For a freedom we further pursue.
We believe in our hearts a new day will dawn,
God's justice will surely break through.

CHORUS

Expansive, Subversive Horizons

The Gospel writers themselves allegorize many of the parables, using them as stories to highlight the salvation wrought by Jesus over against the rejection he suffered at the hands of the Jews—an anti-Semitic interpretation that several scholars today reject. Others have heavily sentimentalized the parables, turning them into child-like devotional stories and feeding the spiritual codependency that afflicts many contemporary Christians. Discerning how the parables mark a coming-of-age then and now, I offer a brief overview of two Gospel parables, the first highlighting the embedded cosmic interdependence that characterized Jesus's worldview, and the second highlighting the subtle subversive transformation characterizing several of the narratives. Both stories also help to illuminate the archetypal wisdom that informs the bedrock tradition of our Christian faith:

> Jesus said to them, "Which of you, if you go to a friend at midnight, and tell him, 'Friend, lend me three loaves of bread, for a friend of mine has come to me from a journey, and I have nothing to set before him,' and he from within will answer and say, 'Don't bother me. The door is now shut, and my children are with me in bed. I can't get up and give it to you'? I tell you, although he will not rise and give it to him because he is his friend, yet because of his persistence, he will get up and give him as many as he needs." (Lk. 11:5–8)

Luke actually allegorizes this parable, using it as a rationale for persistent prayer. In its foundational meaning, it is a parable of Jewish hospitality, with the earth itself deeply insinuated in the ensuing message. In the Palestine of Jesus's time, people often preferred to travel after dark in order to avoid the heat, and visitors would often arrive unannounced. No matter what time of day or night a visitor arrives, the Jewish norms of hospitality require that you attend to the person's need (Gen. 18:1–8; Heb. 13:2). There is no question of refusing. For a host to be unable to offer hospitality to a guest would be shameful; more importantly, it would bring shame *upon the entire village.* A guest is a guest of the community, not just of the individual, and to comply with the cultural (and religious) expectations, a guest must leave the village with a good feeling about the hospitality offered—not just by individuals but by the village-as-community.

The master of the house is known as the *householder,* often portrayed in popular Christianity as the boss, the breadwinner, the person in charge. In fact, in the ancient Jewish context his primary responsibilities were not those we attribute to a patriarchal, parental overseer. His responsibilities for care, provision, and protection extended beyond his immediate house (home) to the entire village.

The Greek word for house or household is *oikos,* from which is derived words such as *ecology, economy,* and *ecumenism.* The Lukan parable referred to above illustrates very clearly the cultural and spiritual significance of the *oikos.* It denotes the house in which homemaking takes place, but the hospitality required for empowering homemaking embraces the larger cultural unit, called the *village,* and that in turn links everybody with the larger ecological domain, typically described as the *bioregion.*

The sociological structure, therefore, is that of an interrelational web, in which the person obtains identity by belonging to a household, which in turn belongs to the village (what today we would call the bioregion), which itself belongs to Planet Earth (not yet carved into nation-states). The parable portrays an integration transcending humans and embracing even the earth itself.

In this primordial, sacred understanding, the nation-state has no place; that is a later patriarchal development. We must also avoid any hint of hierarchical ordering. We are not dealing with a linear construct from the individual person right up through house and village to the planet and ultimately to God as the creator of all. We are witnessing a holarchical, egalitarian process, with an underlying dynamic of empowerment, rather than promoting or fostering anything to do with hierarchical power.

Holarchy is a relatively new concept for our time. The term was originally coined by philosopher Arthur Koestler (1967), referring to a special type of organizational structure in which wholes and parts operate interdependently, following the scientific principle that the whole is greater than the sum of the parts, and yet the whole is contained in each part.[4] This holarchical construct is illustrated in the web of belonging beginning with the *oikos* (household), and embracing the entire universe itself.

The World Council of Churches brought the term "household of the world," or *oikoumene*, to the fore, and in 1991 its former general secretary Konrad Raiser suggested that the word *oikos* denotes "community, webs of relationships, belonging, and with life together" (87–88). The ancient *oikos* is not just one social and economic forum among others but rather the basic social and economic structure not only for the ancient world and the New Testament but presumably for every preindustrial sedentary culture as well.

Also worthy of note is the astute observation of historian Kate Cooper (2013) that three faith-structures flourished in the time of Jesus—namely, the temple, the synagogue, and the household—and in the case of the third, it was women rather than men who provided dynamic leadership (16–17), an observation for which Osiek

---

[4] Biologists often talk of nested hierarchies, sections within larger sections, as symbolized in the Russian doll. It seems to me that what is being described are holarchies, not hierarchies. Strictly speaking there are no hierarchies in God's creation. Everything is programmed to relate—through holarchies.

and MacDonald (2006, 144ff.) furnish detailed elaboration. In fact, several scholars maintain that in rural Galilee during the time of Jesus, the synagogue was not a churchlike entity set apart, but was typically based in a family household. And whereas men frequently cast in the patriarchal line represent the temple and synagogue, it seems that women (and occasionally couples, like Prisca and Aquila [Rom. 16:3; 1 Cor. 16:19], Andronicus and Junia [Rom. 16:7], and Philogus and Julia [Rom. 16:15]) are the leading facilitators of the house-church in early Christian times.

This organic relational paradigm is foundational to how creation operates at every level, very different from the patriarchal carving of the earth into nation-states (most of which were created through the violence of warfare), and significantly at variance with the cold rationalism of mainstream science that views creation as a collection of discreet entities, a material object created for human benefit and usufruct. While this scientific understanding may have contributed to human progress, we are now realizing that it has happened at a high price for other organic species, including humans.

Back to the parable! Beyond the memorable *story* of the late-night traveler, seeking food, the parable embellishes that basic, simple plot into an expansive vision with several layers of personal, ethical, and planetary engagement. In its ecological aspect, the *oikos* flourishes on a delicate balance of several chemical and organic processes. In its economic aspect, the household is a continual reminder to us of the essential giftedness of everything that endows life with meaning and purpose. In its ecumenical significance, the household is not meant to be an isolated entity vying competitively with every other reality, but rather a collaborative endeavor that celebrates spiritual commonalities rather than religious differences. And in its political significance, the household is seriously undermined by subverting and fragmenting creation into nation-states. Hospitality is the key challenge, but of a quality that engages person and cosmos alike—a major challenge for a gospel coming-of-age.

Transgression for Economic Justice

The hope that engenders the parable breakthrough carries an inevitable ambiguity, something akin to the ambivalence described in postcolonial theory. We note this in the often misconstrued parable of the Talents (Matt. 25:14–30), frequently proclaimed within a capitalistic context, with God rewarding the exploitive hoarders and condemning the one who chose not to collude with the imperial system. On a surface interpretation, the person with the one talent certainly seems ambivalent, even cowardly—until we investigate more deeply and see the malicious power games being enacted.

Even a child could remember the parable of the Talents as outlined in Matthew 25:14–30. In Matthew's telling, though, what we have is an *allegory*, not a *parable*. And preachers across the centuries have sermonized eloquently on the allegorical message, reminding us to use our talents wisely, indicating the price we will have to pay if we fail to do so.

It is unlikely that Jesus told the story in terms of human talents and our responsibility to use them wisely. For a start, the word *talent* had a different meaning in the culture of Jesus's time. In its original historical context, "talent" denoted a financial measurement, the equivalent of twenty years' wages for an average worker. Five talents, therefore, amounts to one hundred years' wages, while two talents equals forty years' wages. And let's not forget that the parable is being told in a social context where the vast majority of people don't have the security of even an annual wage; moreover, the prospect of making a profit as we understand it today was largely unknown.

The second cultural feature to consider, largely incomprehensible amid our modern capitalistic value system, is that many of the early Western philosophers—including Plato, Aristotle, Cato, Cicero, Seneca, and Plutarch—were critics of usury (profit-making). In the legal reforms of the Roman republic (340 BCE), usury and interest were banned. However, in the final period of the republic, the practice was common. Under Julius Caesar (49–44

BCE), a limit of 12 percent was imposed due to the great number of debtors, and under Justinian law the legal limit for interest was set between 4 percent and 8 percent. Even the Romans denounced excessive profiteering, which highlights the highly subversive nature of the parable of the Talents in its unambiguously denouncing the empire, its greed, and exploitation.

Now imagine yourself among the people hearing this parable. Bring as much as you can of your creative imagination to the narrative context. Situate yourself among a group of people carrying the onus of frequent tax payments to the Roman invaders along with frequent contributions for the priestly maintenance of the Temple. These are the same people who, year after year, see more and more of their crops and land produce auctioned off as tax payments. And many are wondering when and where it will end; will they be able to hold on to their land, or might a day come when that will also be confiscated? Will they be able to feed themselves and their dependents? Will the male folk be able to find some kind of meaningful work, without which life can become frightening in the extreme?

Many of these people may not be educated in any formal sense, but they are richly endowed with organic agrarian wisdom. They probably know their Hebrew Scriptures better than we often acknowledge. They know what usury means, and they are quick to recognize when it is being flaunted and abused. And the very suggestion that somebody makes a profit to the tune of 100 percent is utterly disgusting; it provokes outrage and anger—the very sentiments Jesus is trying to evoke.

We are dealing with a highly subversive narrative eliciting shock and disgust in the hearers, encouraging them to become proactive in the pursuit of ecojustice (more in Herzog 1994). The alternative they are offered—the person with the one talent—is indeed ambivalent, but with a prophetic twist that enhances further the subversive intent. He chooses not to collude with the financial exploitation. He opts to become the whistle-blower, calling the brutal landlord to accountability while exposing the shameful, underhanded tactics: "You reckless bastard: you sow from where you have not reaped and gather from where you have not scattered"—language that sounds remarkably similar to the prophet Jeremiah.

Over the centuries, this third guy has been maligned and condemned as the waster of the precious talent. Once again, let's locate ourselves imaginatively in the cultural context among hearers of the parable, probably hearing it in their native Aramaic. How does one bury the equivalent of fifteen years' wages in the ground? We are dealing with a cartload of gold or silver. It is not just a case of hiding a small quantity of money to keep it safe—which a lot of people would have done at that time. Although no textual clue indicates another interpretation, I wish to suggest that the subversive vision of the parable is much better served by describing the third person's response as that of *investing the money in the land*—exactly what the Torah required and recommended. Now the one commonly portrayed as lazy and fearful emerges as a prophetic liberator with cutting-edge potential. Of course, he will pay the ultimate price, but his story becomes part of the dangerous memory that in time will undermine even the mighty empire itself.

❄

Personal Reflection

When I first began writing on parables, my attempts at understanding went through several levels of research and comprehension. Having read various commentaries and reviewed a range of different perspectives, I was still often left with a sense of missing out on something much more foundational. On one occasion, as I was wrestling with the parable of the Pharisee and the Publican in the Temple (Lk. 18:9–14), I experienced an intuitive urge to engage the parable through the medium of poetry. It was one of those moments of archetypal awakening that I cherish to this day.

It strikes me that the parables are archetypal stories that evoke a fierce awakening in the hearers. The intention of the narrator seems to be one of shaking people out of complacency, particularly seeking to transcend the numbness of spirit that is consequent upon the disempowerment of oppression. The great Brazilian reformer Paulo Freire called it the pedagogy of the oppressed, which Scripture scholar William Herzog seeks to reclaim as the strategy Jesus might well have used when employing the parable narratives.

Volumes have been written about Jesus's parables, with divergent views on their interpretation. Throughout much of Christendom we have sought to make the parables simple, and particularly accessible for children to understand, which I consider a very dangerous, even an idolatrous, accommodation. The parables were likely never intended for children but rather for adults coming of age, invited to engage the demoralizing powers of oppression and exploitation. These stories are dangerously disturbing, ultimately aimed at liberation and empowerment of all who feel weighed down by injustice and powerless.

Scholars will probably never come to terms with the vision of the parables, and neither will the hearers. At stake is an unceasing invitation to transgressive engagement and subversive empowerment. At the scholarly level, a multidisciplinary mode of understanding will be necessary. For others, the first challenge is to transcend the literary, rational outline of the story. To get to the parabolic wisdom we must plunge deeper, and I have found poetry to be immensely useful in accessing the deeper truth, discerning the call to Christian action, and allowing myself to be lured into the subversive empowerment that many if not all the parables seem to have as a central feature.

❋

The Parable of the Prophetic Whistleblower

The preachers denounce me and moralists trounce me.
They judge me unfaithful, a traitor to power.
A vilified agent and the money I wasted.
I have lived in the shadows of awful repute.
Despite the rejection, no roof nor protection,
I stand by my choice the whistle to blow.
I'm anticorruption and against exploitation.
I don't play the games of financial repute.
It's time for some testing of the Capital system,
The reckless increasing of money to score.
The joy of their master means justice disaster
As the prowlers of profit consume all before.

I waste not nor squander, and my spending I ponder.
I sow where I reap, it's the best I can do.
But the Capital savage must pursue the ravage
And scapegoat the one whose whistle he blew.
The Jesus who spoke it and the Church that invoked it
Have failed to connect to the heart of the tale.
To call the subversive and remain decisive
Was the message of Jesus in original lore.
Like wealth that allures us, the story pursues us.
The subversive truth we oft domesticate.
But the New Reign of Jesus marks another excursus
Where the one with the whistle holds a prophetic place.

By confusing the parable with the allegory, we end up endorsing the voracious capitalistic system described above. But now
we can see more clearly the subversive irony and sarcasm of the
words "enter into the joy of your master" (Matt. 25:21, 23). The
reckless profiteers at the time would have been known as *retainers*—

effectively, entrusted slaves. Even though they themselves had been subjected to the humiliation of slavery, in the hope of making good they often treated their own people as slaves. Yet no matter how much profit they made, or how many of their own folk they cowed into submission, they never rose above the level of being slaves, and as such they were still vulnerable to exploitation and dismissal. *There is no joy for them.* The words are pure sarcasm, in the service of subversive speech.

The evangelists themselves seem to have largely missed the subversive, empowering, liberating message of the parables. Perhaps they knew Jesus's original intent but found it too explosive to retain; instead, they opted for the safer, milder engagement of the allegory. But in our doing so, we have betrayed the creative political and economic pedagogy of the oppressed. Amid the complexities of the sociopolitical and economic world of our time, we Christians also fail significantly. We lack that daring, prophetic creativity so foundational to our human coming-of-age and to our Christian witness.

Parables and the Land

In the Hebrew Scriptures, land carries a very different significance from that informed by the commodification and consumerism of our time. The land is God's primary gift to the people, not merely as a resource for daily nourishment but as an enduring covenantal symbol of God's perpetual faithfulness—and the reciprocal accountability He requires from the people. Thus, Scripture scholar David A. Fiensy (2014) observes,

> Since the land is really God's, no one can sell or buy another's inherited ground in perpetuity. Land cannot be a commodity to be bought or sold at will. Land is God's gracious gift to his people, and thus no one has the right to impoverish someone else. One's land must be returned at least by the time of the Jubilee, and one's indebtedness

must be forgiven in the Sabbatical Year. Thus care for the land is based ultimately on God's ownership of the land. (153)

As already indicated, many of the parables focus on the land, its usurpation by foreign domination, and the ecojustice required for its Torah-based retrieval. For the retrieval in question, Edward Said (1993) makes an astute observation on the critical role of imagination:

> If there is anything that radically distinguishes the imagination of anti-imperialism, it is the primacy of the geographical in it. . . . The history of colonial servitude is inaugurated by the loss of locality to the outsider. . . . Because of the presence of the colonizing outsider, the land is recoverable at first only through imagination. (77)

Awakening imagination is the primary function of all the Gospel parables, and in many cases, the hearers are invited to imagine new and daring ways in which they can, first, expose brutal invasion of the alien occupying force, and then re-vision how the land can be returned to its original legitimate owners. Far from being stories articulating fidelity to a patriarchal God figure (typically depicted as a king), the parables invite rebellion, subversion, transgression, and deviant imagination, to reclaim the stolen land, precisely because it is the sacred space where the people first encounter the living God, the source of their well-being and nourishment.

There are several subtleties in a parabolic analysis of the land crisis in first-century Palestine. First of all, there is the deep desire to dislodge the foreign invader, and the understandable anger and rage when the colonizer robs the land from the person who understands the land to be God's primary gift for the people's nurturance and growth. The temptation to take up weapons and attempt to oust the invader is very strong, and therefore the temptation to collude with the cycle of violence is real (see Crossan 2010, 163ff.), which might be the very reason we need to discern a nonviolent imperative at the heart of many Gospel narratives. Sometimes the strategy used is that of unmasking the violence itself, which is one possible interpretation of the text in Mark 12:1–12:

> "A man planted a vineyard. He put a wall around it, dug a pit for the winepress and built a watchtower. Then he rented the vineyard to some farmers and moved to another place. At harvest time he sent a servant to the tenants to collect from them some of the fruit of the vineyard. But they seized him, beat him and sent him away empty-handed. Then he sent another servant to them; they struck this man on the head and treated him shamefully. He sent still another, and that one they killed. He sent many others; some of them they beat, others they killed. He had one left to send, a son, whom he loved. He sent him last of all, saying, 'They will respect my son.' But the tenants said to one another, 'This is the heir. Come, let's kill him, and the inheritance will be ours.' So they took him and killed him, and threw him out of the vineyard. What then will the owner of the vineyard do? He will come and kill those tenants and give the vineyard to others." (NIV)

Often described as the parable of the Wicked Tenants, Mark's allegorization of the narrative distracts from, and possibly undermines, the subversive parabolic intent. We can no longer assume that Jesus uses the narrative against the Jewish renegades who first reject the prophets and then Jesus himself. In its original context, as suggested by Herzog (1994, 108ff.), this is more likely a parabolic exposition of the violent cycle initiated by the colonial invader but frequently co-opted by the colonized. Such co-option actually undermines the energy for alternative nonviolent thinking, luring the victim into deeper paralysis. The parabolic attempt at surfacing prophetic truth is better accessed by the poetic imagination:

Unmasking the Spiral of Violence

There was once a man who planted a vineyard,
The land he robbed from a peasant farmer
And secured his plunder with a fence of armor.
He molds the slaves into zealous tenants,
And to some entrusts the task of caring
While he goes abroad to exploit seafaring.
But the tenants know that the land they're working
Is theirs by right for subsistence living!
And against the odds they'll attempt retrieving.

For three years running they'll revolt in protest
And outwit those sent to collect the produce,
But the fourth year running they must clench the surplus.
The man's own son, the future owner,
Confronts the tenants to declare his tenure
In a violent showdown, but who's the winner?
The desperation of a brave revolting,
To retrieving the land of divine bestowing!
But the violent spiral has its own undoing.

The elite has force to crush rebellion
And the violent spiral reaps a new destruction,
In an endless cycle that begets repression.
The path to freedom seeks another outlet
Beyond the violence of distorted options.
Nonviolent hope seeks another conscience.
The breakthrough comes at another level,
Beyond the lure of collusive violence,
Awaiting hope with a mystic's presence.

The parables of Jesus invite us into a depth of adult discernment that extends the coming-of-age to horizons that far out-
stretch our lived reality both then and now. This is the archetypal

depth, home to a fuller integration of the personal, interpersonal, political, economic, and theological, all interwoven in ways known subconsciously to millions of people in our world, yet with few credible constructs in either the political or ecclesiastical domains. How to translate the parabolic paradigm into lived reality remains a major challenge for humans striving to come of age.

Another archetypal horizon is spread across the pages of the New Testament and known in the Gospels as the miracles of Jesus. These transgressive and empowering phenomena also stretch our discerning imagination into realms of exploration that rational discourse can never hope to illumine. We pick up the challenge in the next chapter.

8

The Empowering Horizon of Miraculous Breakthrough

Scientifically speaking, there is no reason to want to exclude miracles from the perception of reality. On the contrary, the miracle of the creatively new is already inherent to all processes of becoming. In this respect, one can say: miracles are signs of reality.

—Hermann Deuser

In the period of two hundred years on each side of the life of the historical Jesus the number of miracle stories attached to any historical figure is astonishingly small.

—Graham H. Twelftree

In all, the Gospels record thirty-four miracles attributed to Jesus. These include healing from various illnesses, rectifying disabling conditions (regarding mobility, sight, hearing, and speaking), expelling demons, and three incidents of bringing a dead person back to life. In dealing with the Gospel miracles, we need to acknowledge the various positions adopted by the Christian community and by those scholars, Christian and non-Christian, who have studied this material.

The positions outlined below should not be viewed in isolation. There is a great deal of overlap. Nor does this overview exhaust the complexity of the miracle narratives. Neither the scholar nor the believer can escape the uncomfortable truth that in discerning the deeper meaning of the Gospel miracles we are dealing with a highly complex phenomenon that requires a coming-of-age (in many senses) that transcends both faith and reason as conventionally understood.

Various Interpretative Possibilities
on the Miracles of Jesus

The current research includes at least ten major approaches to assessing the meaning of the Gospel miracles.

1. Across the Christian world, miracles tend to be viewed literally. Jesus was God, and God is all-powerful. God can do things that are supernatural—that is, beyond nature's law—and because Jesus was God, he worked extraordinary, supernatural deeds, from curing sickness to expelling demons to raising the dead to life. For many, the greatest miracle of all is the resurrection of Jesus himself from the dead. Anybody who holds a different view is considered spiritually immature, living in the darkness of sin and ignorance. Here God is understood to be the all-powerful heavenly being, the source and sustenance of all that exists: cosmic, planetary, and personal alike.

2. Closely related is the view that Jesus was the Messiah, uniquely endowed with the divine power of God as liberator and redeemer for all the world. Although the ability to work miracles is not a characteristic of the expected messiah in the Jewish Scriptures, clearly the four evangelists considered it to be so. Australian Scripture scholar Lorraine Parkinson (2015) argues persuasively that Jesus did not consider himself to be the Messiah. We will never know how his contemporaries viewed him, whether in

messianic terms or otherwise. His status as Messiah is probably a postresurrection attribution rather than anything to do with his earthly existence.

3. At the opposite end of the spectrum are those who consider belief in miracles to be a kind of naïve, superstitious ignorance that people outgrow once they become educated in rational and scientific ways of understanding the world. For such critics, miracle stories form part of a mythic view of life, a magical environment into which people are lured because it promises them some sense of escape from drudgery or the promise of a better future.

4. Much of the scholarly literature focuses on historical evidence, with a group like the Jesus Seminar in the USA claiming that no credible historical foundations exist for most of the miracles in the Gospels; even if they refer to some foundational healing story, tangible evidence seems to be totally beyond our ability to retrieve it. Most scholars, however, seem to favor degrees of historicity, based on scholarly criteria such as multiple attestation, coherence, embarrassment, or discontinuity from Jewish views of the time.[1] In the present work, I opt for a third way, beyond the dualistic opposition of historical versus nonhistorical.

✳

Personal Reflection

I opt for a third way also in order to transcend the dualistic split between natural and supernatural, a binary opposition I no longer find useful or meaningful. I worked for five years with the National Federation of Spiritual Healers (NFSH) in the United Kingdom. Spiritual healing is an energy-based modality that distinguishes between

---

[1] Although Catholic scholar John P. Meier consistently employs these criteria, when it comes to the miracles, and specifically the exorcisms attributed to Jesus, he concludes (1994) that few arguments can be made for historical foundations. We are relying largely on philosophical and theological evidence.

curing and healing, the former denoting medical or pharmacological intervention, and the latter describing an improved state of health and well-being arising from alternative or complementary methods.

The state of well-being described under the rubric of healing is known in every human culture—but with a stronger credibility in the East than in our Western world, where rational science has heavily influenced our ways of dealing with sickness and pain. Healing—rather than curing—tends to involve noninvasive strategies, the effectiveness of which depends on the intentionality of the giver (the healer) and the responsiveness of the recipient. There is certainly a psychosomatic dimension involved, as there most likely was in the Gospel miracle wrought on the man lowered down through the roof, whose healing was activated through Jesus's reassurance that his sins were forgiven (Mk. 2:1–12). Was the man crippled by disease or by the weight of a guilty conscience? Was the healing of his inner being (spirit) the actual catalyst for reactivating his bodily mobility?

Two other factors have colored my approach to Jesus's miracles. First comes the sense of Spirit-power that featured strongly in several ancient cultures, with disease or sickness suggesting that people were not genuinely grounded in their relationships with the spirit world. The second factor is a recent field of study known as postcolonialism, which reviews the deleterious impact that external colonization can have on people's health and wholeness, often resulting in a state of internalized oppression (explained below). In this case, the miracle is the healing process that helps to unlock the debilitating trauma.

Having considered a range of explanations for the miracles of Jesus, the one I find most compelling—and, sadly, adopted by very few scholars—is that of miracles as parables-in-action. We then end up with two kinds of parables: those of the word and those of action—all of which reinforces an archetypal view, suggested many years ago by British scholar Nicola Slee (in Hampson 1996, 42), that we should consider the story of Jesus himself in parabolic terms. Thus she writes,

> *Like the parables, the story of Jesus is a story told with a marked economy and vividness of description and evocation, allied with an absence of explanation or interpretation, such that it is the story itself which holds the meaning, and the reader is constantly teased into making his or her judgment about it. Like the parables, it is a story characterized by elements of shock, surprise, extravagance, and reversal, which disrupt the horizons of normalcy and compel the reader to come to decision and judgment. And like the parables, it is a story open to multiple interpretation, thus respecting both the freedom and creative imagination of every reader.*

In my attempt to discern the archetypal meaning of the miracles, and in the ensuing invitation to coming-of-age in my ongoing maturation of faith, I am left with one unresolved issue: the demonization of death implied in a number of miracle stories, particularly the three Gospel narratives of raising the dead to life. Throughout the natural world, death is a prerequisite for new life; this seems to be the divine imprint inscribed at every level of God's creation. Death is not an evil to eliminate. It is not a consequence of sin (as St. Paul declares), but a God-given paradoxical dimension without which nothing can grow or flourish. In a world riddled with so much meaningless death, for me the great miracle would be to see more people die with love and dignity, rather than trying to avoid death at all costs.

Beyond the predominant for/against arguments outlined above, we need to acknowledge a range of other possible explanations.

5. The world in which Jesus lived was inundated with spirit forces that were perceived to control many aspects of daily life. This cultural and religious phenomenon must be understood in context. As I indicate later, this issue is far more complex than religious scholars have hitherto acknowledged. Several exorcisms attributed to Jesus—which Graham Twelftree (1999) claims to be the bulk of his miracles—involve ways of engaging with the spirit world that require a much more profound and nuanced analysis of the relevant data.

6. People endowed with the gift of healing are known to have existed in many parts of the ancient world. In relation to this gift we need to distinguish between healing and curing. The latter is a medical concept largely unknown in ancient times; the miracles are more about healing than curing. The healing in question is about the entire person (body-mind-spirit), not merely about the physical body. Also worth noting is the huge resistance that currently exists in both medicine and religion to the contemporary art of healing, practiced universally by people who, indisputably, are gifted for such a ministry (see more in Marchant 2016; Siegel 2013).

7. Vitally important also is the communal dimension— consistently emphasized by Scripture scholar Richard Horsley (2014). Several of Jesus's miracles are about reconciling the alienated or debilitated person with his or her community. In trying to discern the deeper significance of Jesus as a healer— which Steven Davies (1995) claims to be Jesus's primary iden- tity—we may have much to learn by viewing Jesus as a shaman, as South African scholar Pieter Craffert (2008) suggests. In other words, miracles are not merely about the well-being of individual

people but about restoring right relationships for more empowering communal upbuilding.

8. Psychosomatic conditions related particularly to taming demonic forces take on new meaning today, thanks to the social and psychological sciences. For example, we can explain epilepsy in medical terms and offer a range of pharmacological treatments unknown before the nineteenth century. Earlier articulations should not be dismissed as primitive, but rather acknowledged as congruent with the prevailing philosophical and healing wisdom of the time.

9. Thanks to the extensive multidisciplinary scholarship of recent decades, we are required to transcend the judgmental stance we have often adopted toward ancient peoples, with a tendency to view them as being primitive, prerational, and ignorant. Such peoples were often immersed in the innate wisdom of the cosmic creation, with capacities for imagination and creativity that we have lost today because of excessive rationalism. I cite once again the relevant observation of Scripture scholar John Dominic Crossan (1996): "My point, once again, is not that those ancient people told literal stories, and we are now smart enough to take them symbolically, but that they told them symbolically and we are now dumb enough to take them literally" (79). I suspect that the primary meanings of several features of the miracle narratives are in the symbolic and metaphorical realms, so there is no point in trying to figure out what exactly happened or what can be verified objectively or historically.

10. Postcolonial studies provide valuable insights into the pain and suffering people endure under the duress of foreign occupation. One frequent outcome is that of *internalized oppression*, which can result in a range of physical, mental, and psychosomatic symptoms. Maurice Casey (2010, 258) draws our attention to the fact that many soldiers suffered hysterical paralysis after World War I, and that psychosomatic illness increased significantly after the war.[2]

---

[2] James Carroll (2014) suggests that the Jewish-Roman War (66–

How many of those healed by Jesus were the victims of war-related or violent oppression? For those who were, the miracles have to be viewed as countercultural acts of prophetic empowerment for those trapped in the bondage of colonial invasion (see Pagola 2009, 169–73).

Despite the fact that the oldest New Testament writings (the letters of St. Paul) never allude to the miracles, an abundance of internal and external evidence supports the view that Jesus exhibited unique healing power. He seems to have adopted skills and techniques used by other healers, yet the people clearly detected something distinctively unique in Jesus's approach. In all probability it was *not* his divinity that made the difference, but rather the view that he was a prophet who healed by the Spirit of God—a conviction that may have arisen from the inherited Jewish wisdom around Moses, Elijah, and Elisha. Above all else, it seems to have been the *personal encounter with Jesus* that made the difference. In the words of Spanish theologian José A. Pagola (2009), "The therapy that Jesus applied was his own person, his passionate love of life, his wholehearted acceptance of every sick person, his power to renew a person from the bottom up, and the contagion of his faith in human beings" (166).

The miracles seem to have been a central feature of the new companionship of empowerment, thus marking a coming-of-age characterized by greater wholeness, integration, and empowerment. Therefore, any suggestion that Jesus uses miracles to dominate, control, patronize, or evoke faith in his divinity is unlikely to be authentic. Viewing Jesus as a miraculous guru with superior powers, one who exerts a quality of influence that breeds codependency

---

73 CE)—what he calls the first Holocaust—exerted a huge influence in the writing of the Gospels, particularly the Gospel of Mark. Faced with such extensive and intense violence, and its ravaging impact on the lives of the people, perhaps this explains Mark's strong interest in evil possession and the need to expel the demonic force, imperial in nature, rather than anything to do with demonology as we understand it in conventional religious terms.

in the other, is not compatible with the empowering liberator of the new companionship (the kingdom). Miracles should not be viewed merely as proof of Jesus's divinity, but rather for the mutual empowerment that accompanies the reawakening of the divine power in everybody. In this way, divinity is understood as an intensification of our humanity rather than a status superior to it.

Healing in the Power of the Spirit

In addition to the factors outlined above, I want to explore the meaning of Gospel miracles by further expanding on some key points to which I have already alluded. At the heart of this communal web is the energizing and empowering Spirit of God, integral to the Spirit-infused culture of several ancient societies. One cultural articulation of this spirit endowment—usually described as Spirit-power—is that of shamanism. Unfortunately, the phenomenon tends to be both glamorized and demonized in the contemporary world, with both sides missing the complex nature of the trans-cultural presence of Spirit-power.[3] The late Marcus Borg, who frequently described Jesus as a *Spirit-filled person*, goes on to describe what he meant:

> Spirit persons are known cross-culturally. They are people who have vivid and frequent subjective experiences of another level or dimension of reality. These experiences involve momentary entry into non-ordinary states of consciousness and take a number of different forms. Sometimes there is a vivid sense of momentarily seeing into another layer of reality; these are visionary experiences. Sometimes there is the experience of journeying into that

---

[3] Eliade (1964) is still widely regarded as an authoritative study on the phenomenon of shamanism. I also commend the research of a Russian professor of biology in the United States, Andrei Znamenski (2007). South African biblical scholar Pieter Craffert (2008) provides us with a comprehensive study on Jesus as a shaman.

other dimension of reality; this is the classic experience of the shaman. Sometimes there is a strong sense of another reality coming upon one, as in the ancient expression "the Spirit fell upon me." Sometimes the experience is of nature or an object within nature momentarily transfigured by "the sacred" shining through it. . . . What all persons who have these experiences share is a strong sense of there being more to reality than the tangible world of our ordinary experience. They share a compelling sense of having experienced something "real." They feel strongly that they know something they didn't know before. Their experiences are noetic, involving not simply a feeling of ecstasy, but a knowing. What such persons know is the sacred. Spirit persons are people who experience the sacred frequently and vividly. They mediate the Spirit in various ways. Sometimes they speak the word or the will of God. Sometimes they mediate the power of God in the form of healings and/or exorcisms. Sometimes they function as game finders or rainmakers in hunting-and-gathering and early agricultural societies. Sometimes they become charismatic warriors and military leaders. What they all have in common is that they become funnels or conduits for the power or wisdom of God to enter into this world. Anthropologically speaking, they are delegates of the tribe to another layer of reality, mediators who connect their communities to the Spirit. (1994a, 35–36)

This, I suggest, rather than any messianic superpower, is what enabled Jesus to deal so creatively with the spirit-saturated culture of his day. It also points the way to an archetypal understanding of Jesus (not to be confused with the Holy Man identification), representing not merely the onetime historical (biological) person called Jesus but rather one who embodied a range of transpersonal endowments belonging to a more evolved articulation of human potential. This perspective requires even a larger canvas of investigation, beyond church and formal religion, incorporating the evolving creation itself. This, I suggest, is the greatest miracle of all, the cosmos to which we belong and the home planet that provides everything we need for life and meaning.

In suggesting this characterization of the historical Jesus as a renowned healer, we must not descend into a dualistic split between Jesus, perceived to be all-powerful, and a general population unacquainted with such Spirit-power. To the contrary, we are probably dealing with people who, because of their deep immersion in the organicity of creation, were endowed with a deeply integrated faith somewhat similar to the belief in God as the Great Spirit, as witnessed extensively among contemporary indigenous peoples. In fact, the people's subliminal faith might well have enabled and empowered Jesus to be such an exemplary healer.

Take, for instance, the stories of the Syrophoenician woman (Mk. 7:24–29) and the woman with the hemorrhage (Mk. 5:25–34). The Syrophoenician woman pleads with Jesus to heal her daughter. After the altercation about throwing the food to the dogs, we hear no more of the daughter and her illness, yet the story informs us that she was healed. By whom? Jesus or the woman herself? My vote is for the latter.

And how do we discern the meaning of the story of the woman with the hemorrhage? Imagine what it must be like to spend twelve years rejected, denounced, and oppressed because of a persistent bleeding condition, with the possibility of several derogations related to ritual impurity. Such a person, often being anemic (because of loss of blood), is likely to have suffered from physical exhaustion and debilitating depression as well. Yet when she hears that Jesus the healer is in the vicinity, she makes a beeline for him and pushes her way through the crowd, knowing that if she even touches the hem of his garment, she will be healed. And she *was* healed. How? By Jesus, or her own miraculous transcendence of her crippling helplessness?

In a Spirit-infused culture, contrary to some of the charismatically inflated and exaggerated tales of our time, the Spirit works throughout the entire communal body, including the land itself. The miracle worker is not superior to the group but integral to it. The healing prerogative belongs to all, although it might be more explicitly manifest in some people than in others.

The Communal Context

Assuming the deeply empowering and liberative energy of the Spirit-infused context, we begin to sense a communal raison d'être underpinning several of the Gospel miracle stories. From the Gospel writers we have inherited a portrayal of Jesus as a heroic miracle worker engaging individual clients, with strong echoes of a dualistic split between the powerful and the powerless. On closer examination, we note that the context nearly always involves a wider community, a relational web that includes not only humans but other organic creatures as well. Richard Horsley (2012; 2014) consistently draws our attention to this communal dimension:

> Jesus's role as a prophet in general and his healing and exorcism in particular were relational and contextual and were rooted in cultural tradition. Jesus could heal because the people with illnesses resulting from their circumstances were longing for healing and because they trusted that he could heal. The relational factors were multiple. (Horsley 2012, 119)

How far can we stretch this communal context? The Gospels keep it within the human realm and, at times, with echoes of a dualistic split between the able-bodied and the infirm. In recent times a number of scholars raise grave concern around the Gospel's treatment of people with disabilities—with Jesus himself seemingly adopting the normalization of the human condition in terms of able-bodied persons. Canadian scholar Sharon V. Betcher, herself a physically disabled person and a leading theological voice in disability studies, argues that the miracle tradition of the

Gospels is actually aversive to disabled persons. Concluding that the miracle tradition is a terror for people living with disabilities, Betcher writes (2013),

> The miracle accounts of "the blind see, the deaf hear, the lame walk" (Isa. 35:5–6; Lk. 7:22; Matt. 11:4–5), when worked through theological anthropology and post-colonial-disability analysis, serve rather as metonyms for resisting empire. We today will be challenged to read miracle stories in such a way as to reverse the assumed normalization of bodies, which makes them complicit with cultural horizons of labor and consumer value. . . . Continuing to circulate these stories as accounts of miraculous remediation, or even simply as "healing," contributes today to the scaling of the body for "empire," for globalizing capitalism, for making bodies complicit with consumer capitalism. (162)

Several complex issues arise here, requiring deeper discernment both in terms of archetypal truth and the coming-of-age proclaimed throughout this book. Today, commercial interests are invested heavily in the able-bodied, to a degree that deficiencies in our embodied state—physical limitation, sensory restriction, sickness of any type, old age, death itself—are considered to be cultural evils that we must eliminate by every means possible. Our capitalistic value system has little or no tolerance for human limitation, particularly as manifested in restricted physical or mental capacity. We expect everybody to be able to function at full capacity, all of the time, and when that is not forthcoming we cast negative aspersions, many of which are cruel and even barbaric.

Sharon Betcher seems to suggest that something of this same somatic ideology prevailed long before the present era, even at the time of Jesus. People who were blind, lame, deaf, or dumb were assumed to be victims of a curse or an evil spirit and therefore needed to be rescued from their plight and returned to normalcy.

In this case, the fully abled, embodied person was deemed to be God's only acceptable choice. Therefore, the Jesus commonly portrayed as being on the side of the weak and the marginalized, when it comes to people with disabilities, seems to side with the empire builders whose primary interest is in the able-bodied.

In a book of this size, I obviously cannot hope to do justice to this complex and pressing issue. In the reflections that follow, I am particularly indebted to British Scripture scholar Louise Lawrence (2013) for her incisive analysis of disability in the Gospels. Building on the work of Jewish scholar Yael Avrahami on sensory anthropology, Lawrence (2013) notes that sensory disabilities throughout the Bible are often associated with divine punishment and rejection of opponents: "Divine chastisement for example was often meted out through the senses (Deut. 28:28–29) and warriors too sought to inflict physical damage on sense organs to indicate the loser's surrender and inferiority. . . . The sensory disabled are in effect rendered as non-persons" (15). Quoting from Olyan (2008), Lawrence suggests that disability in the Scriptures is often associated with weakness, vulnerability, dependence, and ineffectuality, creating structures of exclusion and disempowerment that are rarely named or confronted in biblical lore. According to Wendy Cotter (2010, 42), Bartimaeus is the only healed person in the Gospels who is actually identified by name.

Disability in the Gospels is often attributed to human sin, one's own or that of one's ancestors. More frequently, it is assumed to be the result of possession by evil spirits. Much more serious is the tendency to attribute disability to an incapacity or unwillingness to behave religiously. Blindness is often equated with being spiritually in the dark, deafness is associated with an inability to hear God speak, and being unable to speak renders one defective in being able to give glory to God. Both the leper and the blind man rely on others to activate a resolution to their plight, identifying disability with disempowering codependency.

Perhaps the most awkward question of all arising from such considerations is the ambiguous and collusive role adopted by—or attributed to—Jesus when dealing with human disability. We never hear of Jesus embracing a blind, deaf, or mute person simply for who that person is as a human being living with human limits, and perhaps doing so with admirable resilience, often within a culture where the shame-honor dynamic caused serious social dislocation for such persons. Instead of admiring and reinforcing their resilience, Jesus is consistently portrayed as rectifying and eliminating disabilities in order to raise such people to the standards of the dominant culture. Nor does Jesus ever invite such healed people to become disciples.[4]

Throughout the Gospels, sighted people take priority for being enlightened and capable of understanding at levels superior to those lacking sight. Is this a religious/cultural prejudice whereby blindness is regarded as some kind of curse—or worse, a form of demonic possession? In the case of Bartimaeus, a congenitally blind man, we hear the disciples ask, "Rabbi, who sinned, this man or his parents, that he was born blind?" In dealing with those afflicted with deafness and the inability to speak, the disability is frequently attributed to the influence of evil spirits. Obviously this attribution needs to be understood in its cultural context, where many forms of illness were understood to be the work of malignant spiritual forces. We need to remember that such ancient cultures were also richly endowed with ritual resources and skills to alleviate such afflictions. For example, using saliva and spitting were behaviors that many exorcists (read: healers) adopted in addressing human disability.

---

[4] Worthy of note, however, is Wendy Cotter's (2010) astute observation that those who confront Jesus with a plea for healing do so with courage and conviction far beyond what was culturally accepted at the time, and Jesus never disapproves (7–9, 66, 74, 134, 146ff., 254). Cotter (2010) concludes, "The petitioners remain spunky, pushy, and outrageous. Jesus meets them on their own ground and moves to their side, recognizing their need, their confidence, and the rightness of radical resolution when salvation from disease, demons, death or danger is within reach" (256).

As portrayed in the Gospels, the dualistic split between the able-bodied, powerful Jesus and the powerless condition of those with a disability in all probability creates a false dichotomy, one that camouflages and undermines the communal context of Jesus's healing ministry. We also run the risk of literalizing such miracle narratives, thus obfuscating and misinterpreting deeper archetypal factors. Postcolonial studies may enable us to see a way through and discern a more empowering outcome.

Engagement with the spirit world in the time of Jesus was considerably more complex than current moralistic criteria are capable of understanding. By the time of the historical Jesus, several cultures already knew and employed a type of mystical wisdom to engage what today we call the spirit world. This ancient cultural force has been extensively undermined, to the point of being demonized, by the emergence of the evangelists' overly rational metaphysical outlook. We can probably never clarify where Jesus stood on this critical issue, but it seems religiously irresponsible to go on assuming that Jesus fully supported and endorsed the demonization of Spirit-power. That perception is probably a culturally defined one imposed upon Jesus rather than one he himself would have embraced. In the Gospels we are introduced to only one side of the spirit-imbued universe: the negative, destructive side. In an example of classical Greek dualism, we are never allowed to consider meanings belonging to the other half of life.

The Postcolonial Optic

The plight of the disabled in the Gospel miracle tradition may be partly resolved when we review the impact of colonial disempowerment at that time. Here I draw insights from a field of study known as *postcolonialism*, the Christian dimensions of which I outline in a previous work (O'Murchu 2014a). Rita N. Brock (1992), herself acquainted with the experience of personal trauma but viewing it in a larger cultural context, makes this observation about evil possession in Mark's Gospel: "Possession is not the result of personal sin and cannot be healed by private penance. The possession comes from relationships lived under the deceptions of unilateral power" (79), to which Anna Runesson (2011) adds an astute observation:

> Not only do Jesus's exorcisms deal directly with the subject of colonial oppression; they address the problem more to the point than would a straightforward confrontation between the Messiah and the Roman generals. Far from treating the symptom without addressing the disease, Jesus's exorcisms cut directly to the heart of the matter, even if a single exorcism leaves much more work to be done. (211)

Postcolonial studies enable us to uncover the debilitating impact of colonial power that often leaves conquered, subdued people with a range of internalized oppressions, which can manifest as sicknesses and bodily or mental malfunctions. Using this perspective, we can throw new light on Gospel miracles related to blindness, deafness, and other conditions of embodied impairment.

We seem to have two possible avenues for exploring the deeper issues (the archetypal depth) of the coming-of-age that our faith invokes today. One avenue is metaphorical labeling, in which allusions to the blind, deaf, mute, and so on might be read from a parabolic point of view and not interpreted literally. Another avenue is to challenge the traditional metaphysical projections we make about Jesus as the all-knowing, all-powerful One who can never make a mistake.

How many of the disabilities in the Gospels actually translate as external symptoms of internalized oppression, incurred by the disempowerment brought about by political oppression of the Romans and the inferior feelings people internalized when they could not pay temple taxes? In the story of the crippled man let down through the roof (Mk. 2:1–12), Jesus's response suggested that his disability came about primarily because of moral or religious guilt. Once the internalized "block" was removed, the physical entrapment could be released. How much deterioration in bodily well-being recorded in the Gospels is the result of such oppression, in which case the healing is itself a condemnation of the imperial system, and not merely a remedy for disabled persons? This postcolonial interpretation augments the deeper search for meaning that this book seeks to foster. However, a bewildering question persists: why was Jesus not more overt and explicit in condemning the cultural oppression?

This question brings us to a second possible explanation. In terms of his incarnational identity, we claim that Jesus was fully God and fully human. Traditionally, that fullness of humanity has been explained by Greek metaphysical attributes such as omnipotence and omniscience, suggesting that in the humanity of this divine figurehead there is no limitation; there is only complete perfection. But this claim is meaningless in terms of being authentically human. One cannot be truly human without making mistakes and revealing human vulnerability. Jesus could not be fully human if he never erred or manifested the limitations that are integral to the archetypal meaning of what is involved in being human.

We do see Jesus exhibiting the limitations of his human nature—for example, in his derogatory response to the Syrophoenician woman, in his mistaken admonition to the disciples that they would not have gone 'round the towns of Israel before God brought about an eschatological end, and in his all-too-human cry from the cross: "My God, my God, why have you abandoned me?" (Mk. 15:34). If these were characteristics of the all-too-human Jesus, did he also make the error of being seduced by the patriarchal, imperial lure whereby he felt that he had to elevate every person with a disability to the status of the able-bodied?

And for our coming-of-age in a world so intolerant of limitation or vulnerability, contradicting the fragile dimensions of the evolutionary creation itself, how do we discern a contemporary response so that we too don't continue to be seduced by a form of utopianism full of unrealizable promises and rarely if ever delivering authentic hope?

Miracles and the New Companionship of Empowerment

As indicated earlier, I want to reclaim a long-standing conviction among Scripture scholars that the miracles provide foundational evidence for the kingdom of God at work in Jesus's life and ministry. I share the view of many contemporary scholars that the phenomenon described in the Gospels as the kingdom of God is the heart and soul of our Christian faith but has been poorly understood, and inadequately appropriated, throughout Christian history. The miracles should be viewed as primary catalysts for a new quality of empowerment.

Although not always explicitly connected, it seems that the parables provide the foundational narratives for this new reign of God, renamed throughout this book as the *companionship of empowerment*. The parables provide primary insight for how this new companionship facilitates the breakthrough for a whole new way of being in God's world. Moreover, I want to suggest that these empowering, subversive parables of word are complemented in the Gospels by *parables of action*, which we typically describe as the *miracles*. I first came across this suggestion in the work of Craig Blomberg (1986). Unfortunately, few scholars seem to have taken up this fertile, discerning lead.

Several of the miracle stories described as exorcisms are best viewed as parables of action. I invite the reader to revisit material on the parables in the previous chapter. For the purposes of the present chapter I adopt this basic definition: A *parable* is a captivating story incorporating a hidden, subverted meaning that the adult hearer must discover for oneself. It transcends rational logic, unearthing meaning at a deeper, archetypal level. So what might a miracle story look like as a parable of action?

As an example, I use the story of the Gerasene demoniac, recorded in Mark 5:1–20. Jesus is confronted by a man deemed to be possessed by an unclean spirit. Attempts have been made to constrain him, using fetters and chains, which he has ripped apart. His strength is ferocious. He seems to spend much of his time in a deserted burial place, possibly reflecting a popular belief at the time that demons haunted deserted places and usually resided in tombs, but also possibly recalling the words of Isaiah 65:5: "Living among the graves and spending the night in caverns, eating swine's flesh." The demoniac also seems to be into self-harming and wild, frenzied behavior.

Upon encountering Jesus, the man worships Jesus and acknowledges him to be the Son of the Most High God.[5] With a tenor of fear, he asks that Jesus not torment him. Jesus asks his name, and the reply is, "Legion, for we are many." Knowing the demon's name was considered essential to gain control over the evil force, Jesus then seems to enter into a kind of dialogue with the demoniac about the demoniac's destiny after he has been expelled from the man's body. This culminates in the transfer of the evil spirit into a herd of some two thousand pigs, which rush down the hill into the sea and are drowned.

Next, we are told, the demoniac is healed, clothed, and at peace, so enthralled with his restored state that he beseeches Jesus to let him become a companion (disciple). Instead, Jesus instructs him to go home to his friends—thus becoming reintegrated with his community—and the man spreads the good news among his own folks, winning the admiration and faith of many. Paradoxically, they ask Jesus himself to leave the territory; the people now seem to fear him rather than feel assured by his healing power.

This is the story as narrated in Mark's Gospel. And what we have in the Gospel is a *story*, not a *parable*. If we interpret the

---

[5] In this context, addressing Jesus as "Son of God" may simply indicate a faithful Jew, not a designation of the second person of the Trinity, which would have been a much later usage (see Casey 2010, 249).

story as a parable, we must begin to uncover the hidden, sub-verted meaning evoked by adult faith (another nuance for the coming-of-age being explored in the present work). We need to acknowledge that we must transcend the story's literalism in order to access the parable's metaphorical complexity. For example, several commentators draw our attention to the military type of language that Mark employs. "Legion" describes a cohort of Roman soldiers, four thousand to six thousand in size; the term *agele* that the writer uses for a herd of pigs is often used to denote a gaggle of new recruits for the military; the Greek term *epetrepsen* (he dismissed them) echoes a military command; and the pigs' charge (*ormesen*) into the sea sounds like a military attack, all of which gives us a vital clue to the likely context. It might well be that of a man who had lost everything—land, home, family, future prospects—either because of involvement in a peasant revolt against Roman rule, or who by sheer ill luck fell afoul of the worst fortune of the imperial system. To use modern jargon, it drove him insane in the end. Is it any wonder he has ended up in such a demented, tortured state?

The reference to the pigs infected by the demons and rushing headlong into the sea is symbolic material open to several possible interpretations, but once again a military or imperial context seems persuasive. Maurice Casey (2010, 243) claims that the writer is consciously drawing on the fact that the tenth legion, Legio Decem Fretensis, stationed initially in the province of Syria, had a boar as one of its symbols. The notion of pigs running headlong like a herd has never been noted in close observation of porcine behavior. We seem to be dealing with a parable about the unwanted presence of the Roman legions. They, of course, would not have wanted to be sent out of the country, but many Jews would have wanted to see them driven into the sea. One wonders if an earlier version of this story had the theme of driving out the Romans as the crucial issue.

In fact, Jesus's preoccupation with evil forces, and his clear desire to rid the world of such oppression, needs a more imaginative reconstruction (as suggested by Pagola 2009, 169–73). Let's not rush in with the familiar solution of exorcism, or in more recent usage, the notion of deliverance. The Gospels give several hints that evil spirits represent unmet needs, whether understood in personal or systemic terms. The spirits inhabit the inner empty shell caused by feelings of inferiority, unworthiness, disempowerment, torture, pain, and alienation. Nothing in the Gospel narratives suggests that these evil forces are the result of wrong or immoral behavior; their power is garnered not from wrong things afflicted people did, but rather from wrong things that have been done to them by the brutal forces of external oppression.

If the shrieks and tremors of the evil forces represent unmet needs, exorcism is not the answer; dealing with the unmet needs is the answer. Exorcism is not the solution; love, compassion, healing, and empowerment are the solution. Is Jesus engaging the spirits in a process of deconstruction, preparing the ground for the reconstruction envisaged in God's new reign, the companionship of empowerment? The deconstructive task is cryptically proclaimed in the words from Luke 10:18—"I saw Satan fall like lightning from heaven"—reinforced by an even more empowering statement: "If by God's finger I drive out demons, then for you God's new reign has arrived" (Lk. 11:20).[6]

---

[6] According to John P. Meier (1994), "The distinct terms 'Satan,' 'Beelzebul,' 'the prince of demons,' and 'demons' have been drawn together into a demonic synthesis. The most natural interpretation . . . is that Satan and Beelzebul are identified as the ruler of the whole demonic kingdom" (462n40). The new kingdom proclaimed and embodied by Jesus brings an end to this evil imperialism: "I saw Satan fall from heaven" (Lk. 10:18). See also Casey 2010 (247ff.). The cryptic saying of Jesus in Luke 10:18 seems to have arisen from the report the seventy had given him concerning their power over demons. Scholars have noted the nuances in the original Greek text: the words "I was watching" is rendered by the Greek word *etheōroun*, the first-person singular in the imperfect tense, which describes a repeated or continuous action normally occurring in the past. By contrast, the word for Satan's "falling" is the word *pesonta*, the aorist participle, active voice: "to fall; to fall to one's ruin or destruction." Putting these two verbs together in

French theorist Rene Girard adopts Luke's statement "I saw Satan fall" as the title of one of his books (Girard 1986). Girard's scholarly interest is in mimetic violence, often leading to victimization and scapegoating. How do we break this vicious cycle? For Girard, the primordial breakthrough has already happened in the life and death of the historical Jesus, who embraced the role of the scapegoat and victim yet did not succumb to its ultimate destructibility. Even though our world grows increasingly violent, the power of the Christ event is so great that the evils of scapegoating and sacrifice are being defeated even now. A new community, God's nonviolent kingdom, is being realized.

Girard's optimistic view is difficult to credit against a background where Christendom has so frequently espoused violent means to crush its opponents. Nonetheless he is endorsing the metaphorical, even archetypal, richness of Jesus's dream for a new and different future, where the prevailing forces of evil and oppression no longer hold ultimate power. The incredulity in this claim is not in what Jesus dreamed of, but in the fact that successive generations of Christians have not taken the challenge seriously. In terms of such gospel empowerment, the Christian community has not yet come of age.

The Miraculous Breakthrough

The notion of the miraculous carries a universal appeal for the millions of people on our earth who are deprived of the resources that make for human flourishing. With little prospect of ever obtaining the wherewithal for such flourishing, it is both comforting and reassuring to know that a magical, supernatural power can intervene and deliver the goods against all human odds. While such human

---

this sentence suggests that Jesus was continually observing the single action of Satan's "falling." In other words, Jesus was not saying, "I saw the definitive fall of Satan in the ancient past, when he was cast out of heaven." Rather, he was saying, "I was watching, I continually observed, in the victories over his minions, the ultimate downfall of Satan."

deprivation lasts, the miraculous will always have faithful adherents, and the codependent God will continue to evoke credulity and hope.

However, there is no archetypal depth in this view of reality, nor is there any real chance of a creative coming-of-age for either people or other organisms. The universe never desired any of its creatures to live at such low levels of flourishing, and neither did God. The fact that such abysmal powerlessness exists is not a divine problem but a human one. We are the ones who created the predicament, and it is up to us—adults come of age—to resolve it. From a Christian point of view, Jesus provides a blueprint, particularly in that hope-filled strategy called the companionship of empowerment. Too many people are still waiting for divine intervention, while God and the universe are waiting on our collaboration.

I have attempted to uphold four empowering horizons within which we can see the miracle narratives in a new light.[7] I considered the *communal context* as foundational for the archetypal wisdom being explored in this book, and the community I have in mind is woven primarily out of the cosmic creation itself. As a miracle worker, Jesus also belongs to this cosmic relational

---

[7] I am consciously leaving aside two categories of New Testament miracles, those related to raising the dead to life and the so-called nature miracles (Jesus walking on water or calming the storm at sea). In regard to raising the dead back to life (as in the Lazarus story of Jn. 11:1–44), such miracle stories require a more detailed treatment of how the Hebrew Scripture deals with the issue of a miraculous raising of the dead, providing a backdrop for the Gospel examples. My primary reason for this choice, however, as indicated in the Personal Reflection above, is to challenge religious believers (and others) to transcend the demonization of death as an evil we must eliminate. Without death there is no life; get rid of death, and nihilism takes over. Regarding the nature miracles, I am persuaded by the conclusion reached by John P. Meier in volume 2 of his *A Marginal Jew* (1994); after an exhaustive treatment of the nature miracles, Meier concludes, "With the exception of the feeding of the multitude, all these stories appear to have been created by the early church to serve various theological purposes" (970).

web, representing not merely the conventional patriarchal Father God but the more ancient, generic, transpersonal life force, which indigenous peoples all over the world call the *Great Spirit* (explained in the final chapter). I engaged the critical analysis of postcolonialism to illuminate the enduring oppressive and debilitating consequences of abusive, patriarchal power, the destructive impact of which Jesus seeks to reverse and rectify in the miracle breakthroughs. Finally I sought to unravel the meaning of the kingdom of God as a cosmic empowering vision for which the historical Jesus serves as a primary catalyst.

David Day (2001) captures more vividly the empowering breakthrough, parabolically described in the miracle stories: "Jesus systematically waged war on everything which destroyed, distorted, cramped, and enslaved human life. Whenever Jesus finds evil in his ministry he opposes it. The movement of his life, its driving force and direction is against evil and for health, freedom, forgiveness, wholeness, and fullness of life" (73).

Regarding the miracle worker, José A. Pagola (2009, 172n51) indicates that a number of contemporary Scripture scholars believe that Jesus himself may have gone into a kind of trance, imitating the demoniac's behavior in order to procure healing, reminiscent of many ancient and modern shamans (cf. Craffert 2008). Contrary to other exorcists of the time, Jesus did not employ the use of rings, hoops, amulets, or incense. As far as we can detect, he did not even call on God, his Father. Jesus confronted the demonic forces with a power from deep within—depth speaking to depth, at a level that defies all human comprehension and yet is humanly very real, as all archetypal awakening tends to be.

We know of no other miracle worker in antiquity who conducted so many exorcisms and for whom exorcism was so important (see Matt. 12:28 / Lk. 11:20). Since exorcisms were so common and Jews did not consider exorcism to be eschatologically significant, it is remarkable that Jesus claimed that his particular exorcisms were so significant. The miracles epitomize a parable-type transformation in which a new reign of Godliness and empowering goodness seeks to undermine forever the crippling disempowerment so often experienced under the shadow of satanic (imperial) power.

The miracles mark a cultural and spiritual homecoming, at least in desire and aspiration, creating symbolic new thresholds for empowerment, inclusion, and fresh meaning. Disease in that culture primarily signified fragmentation of the relational web of life; the miracle story is a parable aimed at reintegration and the establishment of empowering inclusivity. But the onus on such a transformation, at least from the Christian perspective, is not on some magical kind of divine intervention but on a new awakening of the human soul, with a passion for liberating love and empowering justice. In that context, all Christians are called to the mission of empowering healing.

9

The Subverted Horizon of
Female Discipleship

*Desiring to impress his readers in the Roman Empire
with the trustworthiness of this new movement, Luke
consistently depicted men in public leadership roles and,
in order to conform with the empire's standards, kept
women decorously under control in supportive positions.
Having eyes mainly for elite men, he fudged women into
an insignificant background ignoring the leadership roles
they in fact held. . . . Consequently, Acts [of the Apostles]
does not contain a representative picture of church leadership in the early decades. It tells only part of the story.*
—Elizabeth Johnson

*It is not the task of theologians to heal the rupture that
the divine incarnate made in the world we previously
knew; rather it is our task to continue the discontinuity.*
—Lisa Isherwood

Nineteenth-century commentator Alfred Plummer described
Luke's Gospel as the "Gospel of Womanhood." Of the four

176

evangelists, Luke has long been regarded as the one who most frequently alludes to women, giving an initial impression of acknowledging their significance in New Testament times. Moreover, for Luke it would seem that Mary, the mother of Jesus, is the preeminent disciple. In more recent decades, that face-value impression has been subjected to closer scrutiny, with feminist scholars raising a range of more discerning interpretations of key passages, particularly in Luke–Acts.

Mary Rose D'Angelo (1999) provides a useful overview of the feminist reconstruction of women in early Christian times and specifically in Luke's Gospel. In Luke's treatment, she points out, women are often paired with men, either in the immediate context or in the larger structure of the Gospel, with women's contributions often assessed in terms of male prerogative. The stories about women are frequently shorter, and rarely do we hear a woman speak. As Elizabeth Johnson indicates in the chapter's epigraph, women often served in terms of adding to the choreography of the scene rather than being proactive participants.

Luke's negative treatment of women can be gleaned from two passages. First is the story of Martha and Mary. Here Luke dualistically splits the two, castigating the active one (described by the Greek noun for missionary service, *diakonia*) and exalts the passive, pious Mary. As Warren Carter (1996) and other scholars suggest, Mary and Martha are better understood as pairs of sisters in ministry (similar to Tryphaena and Tryphosa in Rom. 16:12 and Euodia and Syntyche in Phil. 4:12). Just as there were pairs of brothers in early Christian discipleship, it seems there were also pairs of sisters, with Martha and Mary as missionary companions deserving equal recognition.

Second, we come to a more serious issue, which, to the best of my knowledge, no Scripture scholar has yet publicly acknowledged—namely, our interpretation of the Pentecost event as described in Acts 2:1–11. In the process of re-missioning the Twelve with the power of the Spirit, Luke either is totally unaware or deliberately obfuscates the primary group who bore witness to the risen Christ and were commissioned to go forth and preach: Mary Magdalene and her followers. Luke is so preoccupied with ensuring a solid apostolic foundation for his two great heroes, Peter and Paul, that he ignores and distorts the more foundational postresurrection witnesses (see Brock 2003 for more elaboration). And why did he choose Mary, the mother of Jesus, to be with the Twelve (in a role where typically she says and does nothing)? Is Luke so guilty about what he is dismissing that he feels he must have a woman there somewhere? He opts for Mary, the mother of Jesus, when in fact he should have chosen Mary Magdalene, the Apostle of the Apostles, as she was known even within the early patristic tradition (more in Haskins 1993, 58–97).

Luke's treatment of women in New Testament times continues to evoke more critical analysis, frequently culminating in negative appraisal. Dominican scholar Sr. Barbara Reid in August 2015 delivered the Presidential Address at the Seventy-Eighth Annual Meeting of the Catholic Biblical Association of America, adopting the title "The Gospel of Luke: Friend or Foe to Women Proclaimers of the Word?" Later published in the *Catholic Biblical Quarterly* (Reid 2016), it provides a valuable overview of Luke's analysis of discipleship, male and female, with his treatment of women deemed to be particularly weak.

Women in Early Christian Households

None of the Gospels does justice to women's roles in early Christian times. By the time the Gospels came to be written—with the Jewish-Roman War of 66–73 CE as a major influence—an earlier strand of women's more direct participation was replaced by a growing misogynistic influence. The earlier coming-of-age, characterized by what seems to have been a strong mutual interdependence between male and female giftedness, gave way to patriarchal modeling, as recorded in the Pastoral Epistles of Timothy and Titus.

The more creative foundational strand of women's involvement can be gleaned from the empowering and proactive roles women played in the Jewish household. In several ancient cultures, the household (home) was a central cultural entity. Described in the Gospels by the Greek word *oikos*, it can translate as *home, house,* or *household*. However, like the cells in the human body, the *oikos* is porous. Energy flows both in and out, morphing into that collectivity known in Gospel terms as the *village*, which ecologically we can translate into the *bioregion*.

The latter term was unknown in Gospel times, but organic interconnections seem to have been quite significant, with women's giftedness deeply interwoven. The *bioregion* may be described as both a geographical terrain and a realm of consciousness. It is a new and different way of conceptualizing the human relationship with the earth and its resources.[1] Significantly, bioregionalism begins with the organic giftedness of the earth itself and invites humans to work within that inherited framework—almost the complete opposite of the philosophy of nationalism, and the modern commodification of creation's resources pursued by megacorporations (globalization).

Bioregionalism is far more integral to the biotic structure of the earth's ecosystems. It also provides a grounding much more likely to satisfy and fulfill the authentic needs of humans themselves. By maintaining our gaze on those values through which the earth itself flourishes, human beings also thrive and have their needs met in a deeper and more integrated way. Thomas Berry (1985) spells out how this happens in his list of primary bioregional (ecological) values: *self-emergence, self-nourishing, self-propagating, self-educating, self-healing, self-governing,* and *self-fulfilling*.

---

[1] The roots of bioregionalism go back to the 1930s when Fredric Clements and Victor Shelford developed the biome system of classification. *Biomes* refer to natural habitats such as grasslands, deserts, rain forests, and coniferous forests shaped by climate. Particular soils, vegetation and animal life developed in each climate region in accordance with rainfall, temperature, and weather patterns. The state of California constitutes ten major bioregions.

Many of these features are central to the diverse roles played by women in Jewish-Christian households. We are not dealing with mere housekeeping (and its several derogatory connotations for women) but rather with *homemaking* and the many skills and competencies involved. When we attend to the living earth as an organic self, with needs and developmental potential, we automatically enhance our own need and potential for growth, advancement, and the attainment of our own deeper potentials.

The early Christian household was very much a realm of female prerogative (see Osiek and MacDonald 2006). Arguing against the popular stereotype of the woman as housekeeper or subservient wife, Carol Meyers (2016) contends that biblical sources alone do not give a true picture of ancient Israelite women because urban elite males wrote most of the scriptural texts and the stories of women in the Bible concern exceptional individuals rather than ordinary Israelite women. Drawing on archaeological evidence and ethnographic information as well as biblical texts, Meyers depicts Israelite women not as submissive chattels in an oppressive patriarchal system, but rather as strong and significant actors within their families and households. In so doing, she challenges the very notion of patriarchy as an appropriate designation for Israelite society.

Typically, the Palestinian woman of Judeo-Christian times was a multitasker—a skilled, dynamic, empowering person, the heart and soul of the biblical *oikos*, whose several functions have been described as follows:

> She sees to provisions and the care of everyone in the household. She purchases necessary materials, secures wool and flax, spins and weaves clothing, provides food, supervises the work of the slaves, buys fields, plants vineyards, sells the produce of the household, including linen garments, and sees to the distribution of goods to the poor and needy. For all of this her children and her husband call her blessed. . . . She is not confined to the house as will be

the case in later Greek idealization. Her domain is domestic in the broadest sense; political activities belong to the world of men. (Osiek and MacDonald 2006, 145)

Personal Reflection

For much of my early life, devotion to Mary, the mother of Jesus, was a central feature. In our home we prayed the Rosary every night, and virtually every act of public worship included one or more allusions to Mary. Devotionally, we beseeched Mary as an intermediary between us and God (or Jesus). Human unworthiness was a major feature of such devotions; approaching God directly would have been deemed as arrogant and a betrayal of childlike trust. Emphasis was on dependency and not on adult maturity, which I now understand to be a central feature of a gospel-based faith.

Our homes and churches were adorned with pictures and statues of Mary typically shown as a white European woman, laced mainly in white garments (symbolizing her purity), with head bowed and hands joined as if in continual prayer. I was well into my adult years before I realized the dangerous and misleading idolatry of these portrayals, not to mention the literalization of the infancy narratives in the Gospels, where Mary is largely stripped of all that was sacred and unique about her status as a typical Palestinian woman.

My first exposure to a more authentic portrayal came with the publication of Elizabeth Johnson's classic work on Mary, Truly Our Sister *(2003). For myself, this remains the most impressive work on Mary I have ever read. What is uniquely inspiring in this work are the three chapters (7, 8, and 9) that describe the historical and cultural context within which Mary lived and worked amid the daily undertakings of women at that time. While acknowledging the patriarchal, androcentric mores that disadvantaged many women, then and now, Johnson provides a detailed overview of the several skilled and empowering tasks at which women were adept: gardening; providing most of the food for the entire family; weaving; procuring most clothing for the family; education, much of which was done in the home—by the mother; health care, especially via medicinal herbs; financial management, often with limited and stretched resources; and prayer and worship, many of the synagogues being house-based. Robust, resilient, creative, and empowering—characteristics seriously undermined by our devotional portrayals of Mary.*

Rightly, in my opinion, Johnson compares Mary to the Great Earth Mother Goddess, not an anemic, obedient, passive figure, but a woman come-of-age, whose prowess and inspiration we all need for more adult faith witness in the twenty-first century.

The Original Witnesses

Increasingly, historical, social, and archaeological research is resurfacing not merely a more inclusive view of women in early Christian times but the daunting challenge of having to face the fact that they provide the original and more authentic foundation for our faith as a Christian people. In their domestic as well as religious roles, women of the time evidence a coming-of-age rarely acknowledged for its empowering potential. Women were the last of the faithful disciples to accompany Jesus in his traumatic and untimely death (it seems most of the twelve apostles fled in fear), and women were the first to witness the resurrection breakthrough, as all the Gospels record:

The presence of the women at the Cross has historical warrants. All four Gospels agree that a group of women kept vigil, standing firm in the face of fear, grief, and the scattering of the male disciples. Women standing at the Cross, or at a distance, kept the death watch, their faithfulness a sign to Jesus that not all relationships had been broken, despite his feeling of intense abandonment, even by God. . . . The fact that they are mentioned in every Gospel eloquently strengthens the argument that their presence at the Cross is historically accurate in general outline. (Johnson 2003, 294)

Mary Magdalene seems to have been the inspiring leader of that faithful group, and Scripture scholar Sandra Schneiders (2003) notes her foundational significance:

In at least one of the first Christian communities, a woman was regarded as the primary witness to the paschal mystery, the guarantee of the apostolic tradition. Her claim to apostleship is equal in every respect to both Peter's and Paul's, and we know more about her exercise of vocation than we do about most of the members of the twelve. Unlike Peter, she was not unfaithful to Jesus during the Passion, and unlike Paul, she never persecuted Christ in his members. But, like both, she saw the Risen Lord, received directly from him the commission to preach the Gospel, and carried out that commission faithfully and effectively. (113)

The ensuing challenge is well articulated by British priest and Scripture commentator Trevor Dennis (2017): "A pattern will emerge whereby it is the women among the disciples of Jesus who truly grasp what his life and his teaching are about, while his male followers repeatedly show a shocking failure to understand. The male leaders of the Church have covered this up for too long. It is time to take off the wraps" (33). And the removal of such wraps is central to the coming-of age being explored in the present work.

For much of St. Paul's ministry, that which is recorded in his authentic letters,[2] women played a major role. Perhaps this is best reflected in the several women named in Romans 16. Just take one example: Phoebe, usually described as a deaconess (Rom. 16:1). She was entrusted with the task of taking Paul's letter to Rome, in which role she is no mere mail carrier. To the contrary, she would have had to read the letter aloud in several Roman forums, explain its meaning, preach on its contents, and answer several questions from the hearers. Here we are encountering a highly intelligent, formidable woman, undertaking major "clerical" responsibilities for the spread of the gospel and the early foundations of the church. In terms of genius and caliber, we need to ask, was she an exception, or representative of other women disciples of the time? I suspect she was not alone, and in fact may be representative of several of the other women disciples of the time.

Church historian Mary T. Malone (2014) claims that women were the major players in that early unfolding of the movement that came to be known as the church. They exercised enormous influence and laid foundations, the value and authenticity of which have not been preserved; in fact, they may have been deliberately subverted. Misfortune befell this movement in the mid- to late 60s. Thus far (to the best of my knowledge), we have no adequate or comprehensive explanation for this eclipsing of women in the early church. I am personally persuaded that the Jewish-Roman War (66–73) may be a major factor in the debilitating misogyny that came to the fore.

American scholar James A. Carroll (2014) devotes an entire chapter to this claim. Outlining the disturbing evidence of what war does to innocent women and children, he claims that in all probability the first Jewish-Roman War undermined the resilience

---

[2] See chap. 4, note 1, above for the contemporary understanding of authorship of Paul's various letters.

and impetus of the early female-inspired development of Christianity, leading in time to the misogynist denunciation we read about in 1 and 2 Timothy and in several later writings of early Christian times.

Of course it was not the end of women's witness. Their subversion broke through every now and again with illustrious visions of foundational zeal and vigor, of the type recently documented by Christine Schenk (2017) in her archaeological evidence from the Roman catacombs, describing the empowering role of women leaders in third- and fourth-century Rome. Elizabeth Alvilda Petroff (1994) and Mary T. Malone (2001) each provides a fine overview of the female mystical movement of the Middle Ages, with such outstanding names as Hildegard of Bingen, Catherine of Sienna, Julian of Norwich, Marguerite Porete, and the many women who joined the Beguine movement. From the 1300s onward, despite the imposition of canonical enclosure (whereby nuns were not to operate outside the monastic structure), a vast range of female apostolic congregations came into being, rendering—as historian Jo Ann Kay McNamara (1996) illustrates—outstanding service to millions of needy and marginalized peoples.

New Archetypal Horizons

A growing corpus of research on women's historical participation in faith development, within and outside the church, is now available and needs no further elaboration in this book. Instead I want to focus on that which is still regarded as esoteric and insubstantial, namely the empowering female archetypal wisdom that has been suppressed throughout several millennia of patriarchal domination, possibly dating as far back as ten thousand years. Scientific research, focused primarily on rationality and objectivity, is unable to acknowledge or negotiate the underlying wisdom, which belongs to another sphere of knowledge—one focused on intuition, imagination, and mystical experience. Not even the Jungian concept of the archetypal does full justice to this phenomenon. Jung gives archetypes too much of a fixed meaning, devoid of evolutionary possibility; it is the very nature of archetypal breakthrough to remain open to the ever more expansive horizons of creativity and greater breakthrough.

The ancient description of womanhood in terms of the *Virgin*, *Mother*, and *Crone* provides a useful starting point for engaging the archetypal depths of the female. This tripartite structure is often traced to ancient goddess worship, frequently misconstrued as a pagan deviation. Paul Reid-Bowen (2007) and Raven Grimassi (2012) claim that the Triple Goddess is an archetypal construct appearing in a number of different cultures throughout human history, and manifesting in a range of individual goddesses.[3] In broad outline, each of the three elements can be described as follows:

- The *Virgin* (or *Maiden*) represents the power of birthing, enchantment, inception, expansion, and the promise of new beginnings and is symbolized by the waxing moon. In archetypal terms, she gives birth to all creation, from galaxies right down to minuscule bacteria.
- The *Mother* represents ripeness, fertility, sexuality, fulfillment, stability, power, and life, and is symbolized by the full moon. In archetypal terms, the Mother is great nurturer, not the one who gives birth.
- The *Crone* represents the waning moon, wisdom, old age, repose, death, and endings that yield not so much to painful termination but to turbulent, reinvigorating transformation.

Several biblical women are best understood in such archetypal terms. Both Adam and Eve carry archetypal import, which biblical

---

[3] Monica Sjöö, a Swedish ecofeminist, connects the Triple Goddess to the Hindu Tridevi (literally "three goddesses") of Saraswati, Lakshmi, and Parvati (Kali/Durga).

literalism and the prevailing patriarchal ethos grossly undermine. Eve represents the Great Mother Goddess, inhabiting the garden of God's creation, nurturing (and nurtured by) the fruitfulness of the garden represented in the trees and their fruits. Most damaging of all is the literalization of the snake. In the ancient goddess culture the serpent is a symbol for creativity and the power of sexuality. It also denotes the process of transformation that leads to healing (hence the snake in the caduceus symbol of medicine). Once again the story in Genesis demonizes the symbol in the patriarchal drive to disempower—maybe destroy—the power of the feminine principle.

This mythic scriptural conflict between the woman and the serpent (often called a snake) has been inflated into the primordial curse, which humanity must endure until the end of time. Here the serpent is endowed with Satan-like supremacy, who lured first the woman and then all humans into an irreversible state of depravity. Although Christians believe that the death of Jesus on the cross brings an end to Satan's reign, the sinful contamination symbolized in the serpent nonetheless beguiles humans for the rest of their earthly existence.

The demonizing of the serpent provides a classical example of where humans lost touch with their primordial, archetypal creativity as well as their complex unfolding as an evolutionary species. According to Udo Becker (1994, 343), the symbol of the serpent plays an extraordinarily important and diverse role among several ancient peoples. It is frequently encountered as a chthonic being, as an adversary of mankind, as a protector of sacred precincts or of the underworld, as an animal having the soul of a human, as a sexual symbol (masculine because of its phallic shape, feminine because of its engulfing belly), and as a symbol of constant power of renewal because of the shedding of its skin.

In China the serpent was thought to be connected with the earth and water, thus perceived to be a yin symbol. In Indian mythology, some serpents known as *nagas* function as beneficent or maleficent mediators between gods and humans, and like other serpents in other civilizations are sometimes associated with the rainbow. The kundalini serpent, imagined as being rolled up at the bottom of the spine, is regarded as the seat of cosmic energy and is a symbol of life and a wellspring of human libido.

The worship of the serpent is found in many parts of the Old World, in the Americas, and in Australia, where Aboriginal people worship a gigantic python known by various names, but typically is referred to as the Rainbow Serpent, said to have created the landscape, embodied the spirit of fresh water, and punished lawbreakers. The Aborigines in southwestern Australia called the mythical serpent the *Waugyl*, while the Warramunga of the east coast worshiped the *Wollunqua*.

In Africa the serpent was occasionally revered in cults as a spirit or deity. In a cave hidden in the Tsodilo Hills of Botswana, Sheila Coulson, an archaeologist at the University of Oslo in Norway, has made several intriguing discoveries of ancient spirituality-worship, including carvings on a snake-shaped rock along with seventy-thousand-year-old spearheads nearby.

In these varied examples the serpent (or snake) is, by analogy, symbolic of energy itself—of force, pure and simple—hence its ambivalence and multivalences. As we move into the emergence of monotheistic religion about three thousand years ago, the archetypal significance of the serpent/snake is gradually undermined and eroded. Throughout the Hebrew Scriptures, the serpent is depicted as a threatening creature. The Old Testament counts it among the unclean animals; it appears as the idealized image of sin and of Satan, and is the seductress of the first couple in the Garden of Eden. Christians have fully adopted this negative, sinful portrayal.

Archetypal Women in the New Testament

In the Christian Scriptures, we encounter some very engaging depictions of the triple archetype: in Mary, mother of Jesus (Virgin); Mary Magdalene (Mother); and Elizabeth, Mary's older cousin (Crone). In the Gospels of Matthew and Luke, Mary is described as a virgin, translated from the Greek *parthenos*. The corresponding word in the Hebrew Scriptures (Isa. 7:14)—which Matthew cites as his foundational source (1:23)—is that of *almah*, which means a young woman of remarkable fertile potential, capable of giving birth not merely to new human life, but to all life-forms throughout the spectrum of God's creation. Noteworthy too is the derivation of *almah* from the Persian Al-Mah, the unmated moon goddess. Another cognate of this term was the Latin *alma* (living soul of the world), which is essentially identical to the Greek *psyche* and the Sanskrit *shakti*.

There is an analogy between Mary's impregnation and that of Persephone's. The latter, in her virgin guise, sat in a holy cave and began weaving the great tapestry of the universe, when Zeus, appearing as a phallic serpent, impregnated her, leading to the birth of the savior Dionysus. Mary is sometimes portrayed as sitting in a temple spinning thread when the angel Gabriel came to her, telling her that the spirit of the Lord would overshadow her and she would be with child (Lk. 1:28–31).

Throughout Christendom, scholars have cited these parallel examples in an attempt to disprove the historical basis for the entire Christian story. The ensuing debate is often superficial, caught in the polarization between fact and fiction. In the Christian story there is little evidence for objective, rational fact; faith does not belong to that realm of discourse. Instead it is begotten out of the search for *archetypal meaning*, and can only be sustained by reappropriating such deep wisdom for a range of new cultural contexts.

In the present work I am addressing one aspect of the evolutionary shift in the twenty-first century, namely the invitation to a new threshold of adult coming-of-age in the realm of faith. In the present chapter I examined the implications for the biblical reconstruction of female identity and a more empowering role. I alluded briefly to the symbolic and metaphorical significance of Eve in the

Hebrew Scriptures.[4] I have briefly outlined what a reconstruction of Mary (mother of Jesus) might look like, particularly in her roles as Virgin and Mother, both of which have been misconstrued because of biological literalization.

The other Mary we must wrestle with today—particularly for the coming-of-age examined in this book—is that of Mary Magdalene. First, we need to clear away the penitential overtones of Mary's alleged link to prostitution, a castigation voiced initially by Pope St. Gregory (540–604) and long discredited by Scripture scholars. Cynthia Bourgeault (2010) handles insightfully and sensitively the controversy surrounding a possible intimate—and even sexual—relationship between Mary and Jesus.

Mary Magdalene will always defy any attempt at a historical portrayal, primarily because we know little or nothing about her as a historical person,[5] and also because her true significance belongs to that deeper realm I describe here as the archetypal. In her, the ordinary and extraordinary are integrated in subtle and hidden ways. Her brand of discipleship includes all the household wisdom outlined earlier in this chapter, but she also seems to have been endowed with a mystical wisdom whereby she entered the soul of Jesus at a depth beyond that of other disciples, a mystical intimacy that is likely to defy every attempt at a rational reconstruction.

Mary of Magdala has been the subject of intense study over recent decades, significantly from former Harvard professor and historian of religion Karen King (2003), who is widely considered to be a world authority on her role in the early church. Despite the fact that the first eleven chapters of the *Gospel of Mary* are missing, it still provides valuable insight into the personality and disciple status of Mary, material corroborated by other apocryphal writings, such as the *Gospel of Thomas*, the

---

[4] Authors such as Dennis (2017) and Gafney (2008) provide other examples from the Hebrew Scriptures.

[5] Margaret George's (2002) attempt at a historical biography is as near as we are likely to get to her story.

Gospel of Philip, and *Pistis Sophia*. The already-cited Ann Graham Brock (2003) also provides a fine scholarly overview of this documentation. Jane Schaberg's work (2004) also merits its place in the relevant scholarly literature.

The tension between Mary and Peter, along with Peter's alleged resentment and jealousy, is a recurring theme in the written sources, with Mary consistently penetrating the more discerning depths. This is probably one of the main reasons she has been sidelined in the Christian tradition, and the major writings related to her have never been given strong recognition. However, as Ann Graham Brock (2003) highlights, Mary Magdalene is frequently replaced by Mary the mother of Jesus (129–39), a patriarchal ploy adopted not merely to diminish the significance the Magdalene but also to buffer early Christians against the powerful role that many women played in early Christian discipleship.

The elevation of St. Mary Magdalene to the status of a first-class liturgical feast by Pope Francis in June 2016 should alert all Christian churches to her emerging significance in the consciousness of our time. The quality of her discipleship is not about priestly ordination or a feminine face for patriarchal authority. It is much more about the adult coming-of-age that Jesus seemed to desire for all Christian followers, of the past and present. Mary's quality of presence, leadership, and discernment mark a long-subverted tradition, the truthfulness of which can no longer be denied and disregarded.

A final example of remarkable female discipleship is the previously referenced Phoebe (Rom.16:1). This woman is chosen (by Paul?) to deliver the Epistle to the Romans. Volumes have been written on this letter, and its possible interpretations evoke a huge range of analyses until the present day. Romans is quite a complex work, requiring a skilled interpreter capable of handling the several critical investigations Phoebe would have encountered in Rome.

In a culture where it seems misogyny and patriarchal domination were quite widespread, we have to be vigilant and more discerning about the generalizations often made about women in ancient times. We can't even assume that the majority were victims of such oppression. To the contrary, many outwitted and outgrew the oppressive stereotypes. Phoebe was a highly intelligent, socially competent, and theologically erudite woman. Nor must we assume that she was an exception to the cultural norms of the time. There were probably many more like her—indeed, all the women, including pairs of sisters, outlined in Romans 16, many of whom may have been endowed with comparable prophetic vision.

Women feature extensively throughout the Scriptures. Most are never named (unlike the significant males), and rarely are they given the opportunity to speak their truth. This legacy of oppression, injustice, and invisibility needs to be named, acknowledged, and reversed. At stake is not merely the restoration of womanhood to a more responsible status, but the prospect of a more dignified identity for every one of us, male and female alike.

10

The Spirit Comes of Age

Expanding All Our Horizons

Everyone who is seriously involved in the pursuit of
science becomes convinced that a spirit is manifest in
the laws of the universe—a spirit vastly superior to that
of man[kind], and one in the face of which we with our
modest powers must feel humble.

—Albert Einstein

A Church that seeks to follow where the Spirit leads will
have to expect the unexpected and be prepared to be
shaken to its core.

—James G. D. Dunn

Throughout the 1960s and 1970s, a movement known as the Death
of God captivated the Western theological imagination. The *Time*
magazine of April 8, 1966, gave front-cover prominence to this new
movement. Although the statement and its meaning are attributed to
Nietzsche, early-nineteenth-century philosopher G. W. F. Hegel had
discussed the concept in his *Phenomenology of Spirit* to highlight the
fact that redemption by the Christian God had lost much mean-

ing and appeal. Although theologians since Nietzsche had occasionally used the phrase "God is dead" to reflect increasing unbelief in God—particularly after the impact of the Enlightenment—the concept rose to prominence again in the mid-twentieth century, with names such as Gabriel Vahanian, Paul van Buren, William Hamilton, John A. T. Robinson, Thomas J. J. Altizer, John D. Caputo, and Rabbi Richard L. Rubenstein among its primary proponents.

For Christians' coming-of-age, the phrase captivated a growing sense of disillusionment with the inherited idea of a patriarchal, divine rescuer, who, when taken seriously, left many believers feeling hopeless and disempowered. For some, the very word *God* conveyed codependence, fear, alienation, and imperial power. As Christians began to discern the deeper meanings of incarnation, it was the closeness of God to the human condition, rather than the fear-filled judgment of a distant patriarch, that began to make more intuitive sense. Much of the nonscholarly interest in the historical Jesus (throughout the closing decades of the twentieth century) affirmed that sense of a radical divine presence, convivial not merely with humans but with all forms of embodied life in the universe. The God of *Shekinah* (indwelling/presence) was perceived to be more real than God the mighty ruling king and judge.

The latter half of the twentieth century also witnessed another attempt at revisioning our understanding of God, this time through a revival of theological interest in the Holy Spirit. The one who for long had been relegated to a third place, subservient to Father and Son, came to be seen as the animator, inspirer, and unifier of all life—human and divine alike. The Spirit moved from third place on the hierarchical ladder to a central position as creative energizer. This shift in meaning is encapsulated by Michael Welker (2006) as he concludes the introduction to a recent compendium on the Holy Spirit:

> Although the ancient symbols of "pouring" and "Spirit baptism" are adequate for the power envisioned and its working, a new sensitivity for the hiddenness of the Spirit

in creation, for its patient working as a comforting, guid-
ing, teaching, and truth-revealing power, can and should be
raised by a multidisciplinary inquiry. It is in "truth-seeking
communities"—both in academic and religious contexts—
that the excitement resulting from the experience of the
Spirit has to be complemented by the discernment of the
spirits. (xvii)

As I indicate in a previous work (O'Murchu 2012), this richly
promising pneumatology (theology of the Holy Spirit) seems to
have gotten stuck along the way. It has failed to embrace the
enlarged horizon of the Great Spirit, long known to the world's
indigenous peoples. With the coming-of-age explored in this book,
I suggest we are now in a more discerning space to embrace this
new challenge.

Personal Reflection

*I owe a debt of gratitude to the Sisters of Mercy in
Australia, who provided me with my first-ever exposure to
indigenous peoples, in this case, the Australian aborigines.
I wish I could have absorbed all the positive features
that the Sisters detected in a ministry that was based on
years of pastoral engagement and mutual solidarity. A
few years later I encountered the Maori people of New
Zealand, thanks to an initiative of the Marist Brothers.
Both of those formative experiences prepared me for later
encounters with First Nations' people in Canada and the
United States, and a growing familiarity with the tribal
cultures of Africa.*

*One issue aroused my curiosity from my very first
encounters in Australia and New Zealand: the several
references to the Great Spirit. It occurred in the languages,
in the rituals, and even in daily conversations. I assumed*

they were referring to God, and in my few awkward attempts to ascertain which God they were alluding to, I began to realize that my Western metaphysical and theological understandings were more of a hindrance than a help. Clearly they were alluding to something tangibly real, and it would take me several years to figure out what it was all about.

Ever since those first encounters with indigenous peoples, the concept of the Great Spirit was like a turbulent wave, undulating in the fibers of my being and teasing my religious curiosity. Almost twenty years later, the urge to make sense of it all eventually captivated my life. I resorted to a tried-and-tested mode of discernment: write a book on the subject!

By this time, I had several valuable contacts, people who obtained relevant information firsthand. Written resources were quite limited. It took some time to reconcile the theory with the cultural expressions. But a few things became surprisingly clear in a short period of time. The Great Spirit was not a transcendent reality similar to that of other major religions; to the contrary, the Spirit deeply inhabited the land, and it was the organic relationship with the earth that released the empowering potential of the Great Spirit. To the average Christian, that sounds like pantheism, an explanation that has little to offer when we seek to discern the deeper meaning embodied in the notion of the Great Spirit.

In broad strokes, one detects three cultural orientations in how contemporary humans relate to the notion of God: (1) take God lightly—fulfill the religious obligations in a good enough way and don't take religion too seriously; (2) control God—either intellectually by trying to figure out everything about the divine, or religiously by tailoring religion to one's individual's needs; and (3)

mystical surrender—allow God's unconditional love to become the primary focus for a meaningful life.

Much of the material in this book relates to the third position: mystical surrender. Beyond the dogmas, creeds, and religious debates, some people grow into a deeper trust in the realization that—no matter how complex or contradictory life is—the mystery we inhabit is fundamentally benign. This marks a coming-of-age that in the past was often associated with mysticism, either in a very esoteric sense or in a more structured disciplined format—frequently associated with monastic living. That same coming-of-age today has outgrown the more explicit religious context and now tends to flourish in a cultural context, wherein sacred meaning is discerned across several areas of life experience, and the challenge is to grow into a more integrated, nondualistic sense of faith.

Rehabilitating the Great Spirit

One wonders if we are not coming full circle, metaphorically speaking. This new mystical orientation, to which growing numbers of older people are drawn, seems remarkably similar to faith in the Great Spirit as traditionally articulated in indigenous / First Nations spirituality.[1] Contrary to all the major world religions we know today, faith in the Great Spirit never suffered from the adversarial juxtaposition between the sacred and the secular, the categorical split between earth and heaven, nor the theological division between Creator and the created universe.

First and foremost, the Great Spirit denotes the *foundational energy* out of which all life is begotten, grows, and flourishes. It

---

[1] Unfortunately, one must also note that several indigenous and First Nations peoples themselves are only vaguely aware of this profound spiritual wisdom. In several cases, the missionary endeavors of both Christians and Muslims have distorted the foundational truths of this ancient belief and often left the indigenous peoples themselves confused and ambivalent.

knows neither beginning nor end. It energizes all forms of creativity, including the power to create, which monotheistic religions attribute to a patriarchal, anthropocentric deity (a father God, in the case of Christianity). Indeed, it is possible to read Genesis 1 not as an account of a creating father figure but as the awakening, animating work of the Great Spirit, who cocreates out of the depths (*ex de profundis*) rather than creating *ex nihilo* (from nothing) (cf. Keller 2003).

For indigenous peoples, the encounter with the Great Spirit happens first and foremost through the living, organic earth itself. This has nothing to do with either pantheism or animism. It is a perception and conviction innate to humans when we live close to creation as integrated earthlings. The organicity and fertility of the land itself are manifestations of the Spirit's abiding and empowering presence. And just as the Spirit never ceases to befriend humans (as well as everything else), so humans are challenged to befriend the Spirit in our creative coresponsibility for the care and development of the earth.

The wisdom needed for this convivial engagement is accessed by indigenous peoples mainly through ritual, not to be confused with Christian prayer and sacrament, in which we try to get it right with God and beseech God's mercy and help. Indigenous ritual tends to be focused on the fertility of the land, seasonal transformations, the gift of food, and the celebrations of earthly nourishment. Indigenous people neither beseech nor seek to placate a distant God. They don't pray to God, nor do they have anything like a Christian/Muslim sense of worship.

Observers are quick to conclude that this is engagement with an impersonal deity, deemed to be inferior to the personal faith of other great religions such as Judaism, Christianity, and Islam. Once again, we fall into dualistic splitting, in this case the opposition of personal and impersonal. We bridge the split by invoking the notion of the *transpersonal*, denoting the larger organic web of life from which each person evolves and without which we cannot have a meaningful existence.

As indicated in chapter 6 above, we need a thorough reassessment of our notion of the personal and the naivety with which we have appropriated and internalized an individualistic sense of the personal, very much a development inherited from classical Greek philosophy. That same dysfunctional anthropology we have projected onto the many imperial gods that inhabit major religions right up to our own time. In the Christian context, we frequently hear allusions to a personal relationship with God or with Jesus, with scant attention to the projections being acted out, and the often subtle and subconscious desire to control and manage God in our lives. Not much room for a coming-of-age in this codependent relationship.

We end up with an overly anthropomorphic deity, imbued with several Greek projections related to omnipotence and omniscience, to a degree that nullifies the true meaning of incarnation (explored in a previous work, O'Murchu 2017). In the present chapter I want to highlight the suppression of God as Spirit. For much of the Christian era, the Holy Spirit, the third person of the Holy Trinity, was relegated to a rather nebulous third place and featured only marginally in the evolution of Christian doctrine. Thanks to the enlarged horizons of science and spirituality, the Holy Spirit has assumed a broader meaning in recent theological discourse (cf. Boff 2015; Haughey 2015). To date, however, few if any theologians are integrating the wisdom of the Great Spirit into contemporary pneumatology.

The Spirit in Creation

Within this expanded horizon of Spirit-power—more accurately Spirit-empowerment—the coming-of-age characterizing our time moves in a deeper, more integrated direction. While the traditional depiction of the Spirit as the white dove of peace and love carried a mystical-type attraction, it also withdrew the Spirit's creativity from the organic, breeding web of life and its rootedness in the energetic forces of creation, often symbolized in wind, fire, water, and energetic flow. It also created another dualistic split, where all that was good in creation became identified with the Spirit, and all that was bad (e.g., destructive) was attributed to Satan, the polar opposite. Thus we have often missed the chaotic creativity, alluded to in Genesis 1:2, as the Spirit draws forth new rhythm, denoting a birthing forth, even from the random chanciness of creation itself.

The charismatic renewal movement that spread throughout Christian churches in the 1960s and thereafter marked a significant revival of the Holy Spirit, denoting a new freedom of expression, creativity, and joy in Christian prayer and worship. It became one of several offshoots of the Pentecostal movement, originally springing up in the western United States in 1918 and today flourishing throughout the world as the most rapidly growing branch of the Christian faith.[2] For the greater part, the Pentecostal movement has focused on human conversion and spiritual well-being. Despite some socioeconomic and political engagement, mainly in Latin America, it has paid scant attention to the earth and the major ecological challenges of our time. Pentecostalism has remained largely a person-centered movement.

This same human-centeredness is discernible in all the Christian churches, with the celebration of Pentecost every year being acclaimed as a foundational feast for Christian faith and praxis. In fact, several Christians believe that the Holy Spirit only comes to its full involvement in the world after God and Jesus have completed their salvific work. In other words, Pentecost marks the real coming of the Holy Spirit. In the Catholic tradition, baptism is widely understood as the authentic imparting of the Holy Spirit on each person. Traditional Christian pneumatology (theology of the Holy Spirit) seems to have largely overlooked and underestimated the creative energizing of the Holy Spirit at the dawn of creation—and presumably enhancing that same creative impetus ever since. To the best of my knowledge, the only "faith system"

---

[2] This movement has been extensively researched and documented. For a valuable overview, see Hunter and Ormerod 2013; see also www.atlasofpentecostalism.net.

that truly honors the Spirit's creative role in creation is the indigenous belief in the Great Spirit.

Contemporary theologians such as Pannenberg, Wilker, Wallace, Boff, and Haughey all hint at the Spirit's central role in creation's unfolding and in the ongoing process of evolution. Leonardo Boff (2015) is particularly explicit on this matter: "To fully understand the Holy Spirit we need a different paradigm, more in line with modern cosmology. A cosmological perspective helps us to see the genesis of all things: their emergence out of the Unnameable, Mysterious, and Loving Energy that exists before there was a before, at zero point of time and space. That Energy upholds the universe and all the beings that have been and will be; it penetrates creation from beginning to end" (viii).

In one particular passage from the same source, Boff (2015) describes vividly the energizing empowerment of the Great Spirit, although he fails to name it explicitly:

> Something about human beings refuses to think of things as simply scattered about, thrown together any such way. They see an organizing principle that brings things together to form a cosmos instead of chaos. They sense that a powerful and loving Energy is in action, upholding, preserving, and moving things forward together. They dare to give a name to this mysterious and fascinating reality. They give it names inspired by veneration and respect. What is more they can enter into dialogue with it, celebrate it with rituals, dances, and feasts. They feel it as an inner enthusiasm (from the Greek word for a "god" within). It inspires feelings of reverence, devotion, and worship. (135)

Our Cosmic Coming-of-Age

In the present chapter, I am advocating a new theological horizon, focused on the indigenous notion of the Great Spirit. Of all the understandings of God that the various religions have adopted, the Great

Spirit may be the most profound of all. It transcends the narrow anthropomorphic limits of the current major religions, viewing God primarily (or exclusively) for the benefit of humans. The notion of the Great Spirit seriously discredits the imperial tenor of the monotheistic faiths, namely Judaism, Christianity, and Islam. It locates afresh the creative imperative of the Holy One in the heart of creation itself, thus inviting humans to a whole new coming-of-age as creative and responsible earthlings. Perhaps most inspiring of all, faith in the Great Spirit opens up enlarged horizons of meaning deeply congruent with the evolutionary, cosmological, and planetary wisdom of our age.

The twentieth century stretched our awareness of creation to levels unknown to previous generations. In 1927 Belgian priest-scientist Georges Lemaître, drawing on the work of Einstein and De Sitter, proposed an expanding model for the universe, originating with the big bang some 13.8 billion years ago. Michael Dowd (2009) calls it the *Great Radiance* while physicist Jude Currivan (2017, 39, 85–86) adopts a more Spirit-inspired renaming of the *Big Breath*. Simultaneously, we witnessed the coalescing of three key developments: (1) an evolutionary awakening, expanding horizons of understanding on several fronts; (2) rapid technological breakthroughs, particularly those related to the information explosion; and (3) scientific knowledge outgrowing the limited confines of academia, creating a new curiosity, questioning, and for some a mystical search for universal meaning. Within just a few decades, the enlarged horizon of 13.8 billion years became almost a household term.

As we became acquainted with the age of the universe at large and the evolution of galaxies, planets, and our own earth, cosmologists began to weave a new cosmic narrative (e.g., Swimme and Berry 1992; Primark and Abrams 2006) that jolted many out of their narrow anthropocentric views of life. It felt like the expansiveness of the cosmic age was awakening within the human species—a coming-of-age that was stretching afresh not merely the curiosity of the human mind but the very definition of what it means to be human. We began to realize that our sense of belonging could no longer be reserved to the biological realm, nor indeed to the ensouled status inherited from Greek (Aristotelian) philosophy, which tried to convince us that we were superior to all other beings. We are an integral dimension of something much more ancient, complex, and sacred. And without a deeper grounding in those enlarged dimensions, our lives will remain seriously deprived.

Alongside this cosmic awakening we evidenced a growing sense of concern for the precarious state of our home planet, the earth, initially alerted in works like Rachel Carson's *Silent Spring* (first published in 1962). For many Christians like myself, we had to shift from a negative dismissal of the material creation (as source of sin and temptation) to internalizing not merely a sense of earthly sacredness but, more importantly, our God-given status as earthlings, and the responsibilities to live out that identity in more sustainable ways.

Beyond the call to live more sustainably, conscious of the fragile interdependence upon which all life flourishes, lies the further horizon of an engaged spirituality, very much the focus of the present work. While megacorporations, supported by several contemporary governments, view everything in creation as mere usufruct, objectified commodities, more and more people are beginning to realize that such aggressive exploitation is not merely destructive of the earth itself but also makes a meaningful human future ever more uncertain and precarious.

Mainline religion has long been seen as the foundation for a more ethical and responsible way of living. However, such morality has been largely human-focused and embedded in dualistic splitting between the sacred and the secular. Such morality is not of much use in the complex evolutionary context of the twenty-first century, and formal religions are unlikely to exert moral influence from here on. This leaves us with a dangerous vacuum, which in time governments will need to fill, but neither the voting public nor our public representatives are yet ready for this ethical undertaking.

Reconnecting with the inherited wisdom of our indigenous peoples—and their faith in the Great Spirit—can spur us on to become more involved and engaged in this ethical revival. Throughout the human population a great deal of moral discourse is focused on human rights, with sexual and gender morality a keenly debated issue among ethicists. Engaging and including the ecological and planetary dimensions is still a minority concern and, in several religious contexts, is viewed as esoteric and even a distraction from urgent religious considerations. Despite the extensive exploitation of natural resources and the ferocious attacks on other forms of organic life, we seem to be largely oblivious to the fact that, as a species, we humans are totally dependent on all other life-forms not merely for healthy living but for our very survival.

Over the past few years we have been alerted to the honeybee crisis, with death rates of over 25 percent in the United States alone. Bees perform a task that is vital to the survival of agriculture: pollination. In fact, one-third of our global food supply is pollinated by bees. If bees die out, so do we, and this is one small example of the interdependence that needs to become a central feature of contemporary moral values, and the ethical systems necessary to uphold a healthy and wholesome world—not merely for humans but for all living creatures.

Like several aspects of our inherited religious faiths, our morality tends to be based on the patriarchal control of all creation, associated with God the father, or the redemptive rescue associated with Jesus. A morality informed by faith in the Spirit, in this case the Great Spirit of our indigenous peoples, would be much more expansive and inclusive of all life, planetary and cosmic alike. American theologian Marc I. Wallace (2005) highlights what this spirit-infused vitality looks like:

> The Spirit is the "soul" of the earth—the wild, life-giving breath of creation—empowering all life-forms to enter into a dynamic relationship with the greater whole. In turn the earth is the "flesh" of the Spirit—the living landscape of divine presence—making God palpable and viscous in nature's ever widening circles of seasonal changes. To expe-

rience the full range of nature's birthing cycles, periods of growth, and seasons of death and decay—to known the joy and sadness of living in harmony with nature's cyclical processes and flow patterns—is to be empowered by the Spirit and nurtured by nature's bounty. The Spirit is the hidden, inner life of the world, and the earth is the outward manifestation of the Spirit's sustaining energies. (127)

Elsewhere Wallace (2003) adds, "The world's forests are the lungs we breathe with, the ozone layer is the skin that protects; and the earth's lakes and rivers are the veins and arteries that supply us with vital fluids" (147).

In more theological terms this organic, ecological pneumatology is affirmed by theologians such as Elizabeth Johnson and Kirsteen Kim: "The Creator Spirit as ground, sustaining power, and goal of the evolving world, acts by empowering the process from within. God makes the world, in other words, by empowering the world to make itself" (Johnson 2006, 193). Therefore, "the theology of the Holy Spirit is a study of God's involvement in the world. The Spirit represents the presence of God which is throughout the whole creation" (Kim 2007, 15).

Toward a New Integration

In this coming-of-age, three dimensions coalesce, evoking a new threshold for theological integration:

1. *God.* Transcendence and immanence are integrated as the informationally informed basis of what physicist Jude Currivan (2017) describes as a cosmic hologram. This inspirited (divine) immanence is the wisdom that holds all as one and flourishes in a vast canopy of diverse creativity. This is neither pantheism nor panentheism. It is mystery at home in the evolving creation—without beginning or end.

2. *Creation.* As an evolutionary process, creation draws its primary raison d'être from the lure of the Spirit, lying up ahead

and not merely the Darwinian sequence that builds on past successes—a thesis uniquely articulated by John F. Haught (2017). Humans need a transliteralist and transrational mode of discernment and wisdom to comprehend this evolutionary unfolding, an intellectual and spiritual mode of apprehension largely unknown in either the secular or religious sciences.

3. *The human.* As indicated in previous chapters, humans are defined by their capacity to belong, and it is from within this culture of belonging that we discover—time and again—our true nature. We belong to the earth, to creation, and to the Spirit that energizes all life-forms. We control nothing. At every level of our being we are interdependent creatures, and therein lies our uniqueness and our greatness—a cosmic status requiring a coming-of-age that, as yet, very few humans have known in our time.

Many contemporary visionaries are already engaging this brave, new horizon, stretching even our understanding of God. I conclude this chapter with a quote from Beverly Lanzetta (2018), a contemporary exponent of global spirituality integrated with ancient contemplative practice. Although she never alludes explicitly to the notion of the Great Spirit, what it would mean to live by the guidance of this Spirit is illuminated throughout her written works, and nowhere more clearly than in this quotation:

> A new revelation or universal story is necessary to guide our world today, one that respects the biodiversity of life, tapestry of human cultures, and wide expanse of the cosmos. We need to imagine our world in its sacred and prophetic dimensions, in the virtues of all religions and spiritual traditions that are part of our collective inheritance, and in the dignity of all species and life-forms. We need to recover the ancient vision of wholeness and closeness to nature that sustained countless generations, and at the same time broaden and deepen this vision beyond local, tribal, or national boundaries to include the entire Earth community and the cosmos. (129)

Epilogue

On the Wave of a Synthesis

Humanity is being taken to the place where it will have to choose between suicide and adoration.
—Pierre Teilhard de Chardin

An author is always grateful when some inspiring visionary provides a synthesis that serves so elegantly to conclude a written work. Here I quote from Elizabeth Johnson (2014), a cherished friend, and more significantly an outstanding theologian of our time:

A flourishing humanity on a thriving planet, rich in species in an evolving universe, all together filled with the glory of God: such is the vision that must guide us at this critical time of Earth's distress, to practical and critical effect. Ignoring this view keeps people of faith and their churches locked into irrelevance while a terrible drama of life and death is being played out in the real world. By contrast, living the ecological vocation in the power of the Spirit sets us off on a great adventure of mind and heart, expanding the repertoire of our love. (286)

207

This quote captivates the central elements that characterize the coming-of-age I am investigating. These elements include the following:

• *A human species capable of flourishing, thriving, and evolving.* Note, however, that this is only possible in the context of other species with whom we share Planet Earth, and all transpiring within the context of the evolving universe. The coming-of-age described throughout this book is a multifaceted process, a relational, interdependent entanglement of person, planet, and cosmos. And throughout that grand adventure, nothing is static. All is destined for the never-ceasing becoming called forth by the evolutionary lure of the future.

If this interpretation is correct—and I certainly believe it is—then evolution is inviting us to forgo and outgrow the dysfunctional anthropology that has held us captive for far too long. In the oft-quoted words of Marianne Williamson, frequently employed by the late Nelson Mandela, it is our greatness that haunts us, because we have been playing small for far too long. Religion has indoctrinated us into the moralistic codependency of forever seeking mercy from a wrathful God, while our politics and economics have molded us into systemic functionaries serving a human addiction to conquer and control the evil, materialistic world. And our educational systems, co-opted by patriarchal power and capitalistic economics, ensure that we turn out (for the greater part) to be loyally deluded in our allegiance to what is essentially a culture of death.

As a species we have been co-opted into behaving like well-adjusted zombies. The major socioeconomic system has us exactly where it wants us to be: subservient, deluded, dysfunctional, and highly "productive." But productive for what? Not for flourishing, thriving, and evolving in the long term, which is precisely what the coming-of-age is trying to reawaken. We are being lured, often dragged along, toward a new consciousness. Will we make it through? Time alone will tell.

• *Filled with the glory of God.* As Elizabeth Johnson indicates, there is, and there must be, an alternative anthropology.

How do we realign our distorted, dysfunctional system? In part at least, that raises a complementary question: how do we rework the tradition? In our inherited Christian story, the glory of God was manifested for the first time in the coming of Jesus some two thousand years ago. But for those among us coming of age—informed as we are by science, cosmology, anthropology, and the new insights of Scripture and theology—millions of laypeople either suspect or know that the reductionistic two-thousand-year story makes neither scientific nor religious sense.

The glory of God in our world does not begin with Jesus of Nazareth, nor was Jesus sent to rectify some fundamental flaw that brought death and sin into the world. The glory of God is radiant in creation ever since the big bang of some 13.8 billion years ago, or since multiverses first evolved in the recesses of deep space-time. And in our human story, the glory of God has been radiant in our evolutionary becoming over a time span of some 7 million years (elaborated in an earlier work: O'Murchu 2008). To suggest that there was a onetime idyllic paradise in which we were perfect like angels makes no sense in an evolutionary universe.

In terms of the human species, God's glory is manifest in our evolutionary becoming, which paradoxically we get right most of the time, when we remain very close to nature. When we deviate from our embeddedness as earthlings in the natural world, then we deviate from our authentic identity, and that is what we have been doing for much of the postagricultural epoch, throughout the past eight thousand to ten thousand years. Yet God's glory continues to work in us as the life of Jesus *affirms, confirms,* and *celebrates* all we have achieved as evolutionary beings. Jesus is not about setting right a fundamental flaw, but rather inviting us afresh to embrace our true nature and deeper identity. The Christian program for such retrieval is what the Gospels describe as the kingdom of God.

• *A terrible drama of life and death is being played out.* John Haught describes this drama as an evolutionary adventure. It is characterized by freedom and creativity and the deep paradox of creation-cum-destruction, otherwise named as the recurring cycle of birth-death-rebirth. Without earthquakes and their trails of devastation, we would have no creation to enjoy. This is not a flaw; it is the underlying paradox through which everything in creation comes to life and flourishes amid the recurring cycle of birth-death-rebirth.

What makes the drama terrible is the double delusion that feeds our confusion and inability to respond appropriately. First, we live within a profound ignorance of the paradoxical creation we inhabit, and second, the way we demonize death, featured in every major religion, creates and sustains a crippling dysfunctionality. In our rational entrenchment and the ensuing cultural projections, we have engineered the notion of a perfect deity creating a perfectly fixed creation, a rather blasphemous denial of our elegantly chaotic evolutionary creation. Consequently, death will always be viewed as a deviant evil, instead of seeing it as a prerequisite for the new breakthroughs upon which coevolution thrives. And with this positive and more integrated view of death, the Christian edifice of salvation—through the power of the cross—falls and crumbles into irrelevancy.

The drama of life and death, so central to an evolutionary view of life, is never neat and tidy, but humans who remain closely aligned to our earthy embeddedness have never had big problems with that paradoxical mix—until formal religions came along. Then the elegance became "terrible." Endowed with the imperial power of reason, the tools of patriarchal manipulation, and the guidance of a kinglike God (a projection of our own deluded imperialism), we messed up the whole thing. The consequences are all too obvious in the violent world of our time, and the extended violation of so many other life-forms. "Terrible" is too mild a word to describe the mess we have created.

• *Living the ecological vocation in the power of the Spirit.* So, if God does not rescue us from this mess, what hope is left? The coming-of-age described in this book is the growing realization among more and more people that God will *not* rescue us, because it is not God's problem in the first place. It is *our problem*, not God's. The Christian gospel project of the kingdom of God (what I rename as the companionship of empowerment) models for us the way out of *our* dilemma. When will we become adult enough to embrace it? And what is the renewed sense of faith that will animate and sustain us in that endeavor?

Ours is an ecological vocation. We are earthlings. Without right relationships with the organic world we cannot hope to get anything right. That means, among other things, our need to refrain from treating creation as an object, as a commodity, there for our use and usufruct. We don't own creation; we belong to it. It is the foundational womb of our being and becoming, requiring us to radically revision our politics, economics, and social policies, as David Korten (2015) suggests.

Perhaps more daunting is the revisioning of our faith as spiritual beings. Rightly does Elizabeth Johnson align the "ecological vocation" with the "power of the Spirit." Our Christian Bible begins with the Spirit drawing forth the creative energy of creation. *In the beginning was the Spirit*—not the Creator but the Spirit. The oldest intimation of God known to our species is that of God as Spirit force—what our indigenous and tribal peoples have long known as the Great Spirit (cf. O'Murchu 2012).

Our tendency to anthropomorphize God is a theological postulate requiring substantial reframing. It is overloaded with human projection, based on the notion that humans are superior creatures with superior rational intelligence. In this anthropology, the earthling has been disconnected from the earth, and the earthy awareness of the energizing Spirit has been replaced by an imperialistic anthropomorphic deity. As highlighted by religious critic Wes Howard-Brook (2016), the mystery of creation has been displaced by the mystique of empire.

• *Expanding the repertoire of our love*. All the major religions postulate love and compassion as central virtues. But once again, the focus is on the human, as if only humans can exchange the benevolence and care we associate with love. Moreover, in the religious context, the emphasis tends to be on our need to love God better, and our consistent failure to do so. But as Johnson (2014) intimates in the earlier quote, our "ecological vocation in the power of the Spirit sets us off on a great adventure of mind and heart, expanding the repertoire of our love" (286), then love itself takes on a deeper and vaster meaning.

What we are asked to reclaim is not entirely new; in fact, all the religions proclaim it in one form or another: *God is love*, and God's love for all creation is *unconditional*. The notion of unconditional love is for most of us a fleeting experience belonging to those moments of deep intimacy in which we know in our inner depths a sense of being totally accepted and affirmed for who and what we are. Therefore, the challenge and invitation to live out of God's unconditional love for us escape most people, except perhaps those blessed with moments of mystical consciousness.

For those of us whose faith formation is tilted toward moralistic judgment—whether of self or others—the notion that we could be unconditionally loved by God just feels like some wild utopianism, or worse, an incestuous self-inflation whereby we try to convince ourselves that we don't have to worry about behaving morally. Unconditional love is the most daunting challenge of all, because if I take seriously the fact that I am loved unconditionally, then I too must learn to love everybody—and everything—unconditionally.

This is the most revolutionary force that any culture or civilization can ever encounter. It is the ultimate goal of all authentic *coming-of-age*. It is the energy of the creative Spirit come home to rest in the evolutionary thrust of creation, and in the recesses of the human heart. It is the goal of all desiring and the energy force that holds all together. In that space of deep surrender, we know that coming-of-age—like creation itself—is a journey into infinity.

❄

Personal Reflection

On that note this book comes to its end. But there is no ending, no wrapping things up! The creative Spirit knows no closure, only the evolutionary thrust of infinite beginnings. For many years now I have been inspired by the poetic words of Christopher Fry's "A Sleep of Prisoners," and it seems apt to share with you, the reader, these poetic words that have often motivated me in those life experiences when I was invited and challenged to come of age:

> *The human heart can go the lengths of God . . .*
> *Dark and cold we may be, but this*
> *Is no winter now. The frozen misery*
> *Of centuries breaks, cracks, begins to move;*
> *The thunder is the thunder of the floes,*
> *The thaw, the flood, the upstart Spring.*
> *Thank God our time is now when wrong*
> *Comes up to face us everywhere,*
> *Never to leave us till we take*
> *The longest stride of soul we ever took.*
> *Affairs are now soul size.*
> *The enterprise*
> *Is exploration into God.*
> *Where are you making for? It takes*
> *So many thousand years to wake,*
> *But will you wake for pity's sake!*

❄

Bibliography

Althaus-Reid, Marcella. 2003. *Indecent Theology*. London: Routledge.

Bausch, William. 1984. *Storytelling: Imagination and Faith*. New London, CT: Twenty-Third Publications.

Becker, Udo. 1994. *The Continuum Encyclopedia of Symbols*. New York: Continuum.

Bernstein, Jerome. 2006. *Living in the Borderland*. New York: Routledge.

Berry, Thomas. 1985. *The Dream of the Earth*. San Francisco: Sierra Club.

Betcher, Sharon V. 2013. "Disability and the Terror of the Miracle Tradition." In *Miracles Revisited*, edited by Stefan Alkier, 161–81. Boston: De Gruyter.

Blomberg, Craig L. 1986. "The Miracles as Parables." In *Gospel Perspectives*. Vol. 6. *The Miracles of Jesus*, 327–59. Sheffield: JSOT Press.

Boeve, Lieven, Yves de Maeseneed, and Ellen Van Stichel. 2014. *Questioning the Human: Toward a Theological Anthropology for the Twenty-First Century*. New York: Fordham University Press.

Boff, Leonardo. 2015. *Come Holy Spirit*. Maryknoll, NY: Orbis.

Bogart, Gregory C. 1992. "Separating from a Spiritual Teacher." *Journal of Transpersonal Psychology* 24: 1–21.

Borg, Marcus. 1994a. *Jesus in Contemporary Scholarship*. Valley Forge, PA: Trinity Press International.

———. 1994b. *Meeting Jesus Again for the First Time*. San Francisco: HarperSanFrancisco.

Borg, Marcus, & John D. Crossan. 2006. *The Last Week*. San Francisco: HarperSanFrancisco.

Bourgeault, Cynthia. 2010. *The Meaning of Mary Magdalene*. Boston: Shambhala.

Brock, Ann Graham. 2003. *Mary Magdalene: The First Apostle*. Cambridge, MA: Harvard University Press.

Brock, Rita N. 1992. *Journeys by Heart*. New York: Crossroad.

Brock, Rita N., and Rebecca Parker. 2008. *Saving Paradise*. Boston: Beacon Press.

Brooten, Bernadette J. 1982. *Women Leaders in the Ancient Synagogue: Inscriptional Evidence and Background Issues*. Chico, CA: Scholar's Press.

Brueggemann, Walter. 2005. *The Book That Breathes New Life*. Minneapolis: Augsburg Fortress.

Calaprice, Alice. 2005. *The Ultimate Quotable Einstein*. Princeton, NJ: Princeton University Press.

Carroll, James. 2014. *Christ Actually*. New York: Viking.

Carter, Warren. 1996. "Getting Martha out of the Kitchen: Luke 10:38–42." *Catholic Biblical Quarterly* 58: 264–80.

Casey, Maurice. 2010. *Jesus of Nazareth*. New York: Continuum.

Cook-Greuter, Susanne. 1994. *Transcendence and Mature Thought in Adulthood*. Lanham, MD: Rowman & Littlefield.

———. 1999. *Creativity, Spirituality, and Transcendence: Paths to Integrity and Wisdom in the Mature Self*. Stamford, CT: Ablex Publishing.

Cooper, Kate. 2013. *Band of Angels: The Forgotten World of Early Christian Women*. Cambridge: Cambridge University Press.

Cotter, Wendy. 2010. *The Christ of the Miracle Stories*. Grand Rapids: Baker Academic.

Craffert, Pieter. 2008. *The Life of a Galilean Shaman*. Eugene, OR: Cascade Books.

Crossan, John Dominic. 1991. *The Historical Jesus*. San Francisco: HarperSanFrancisco.

———. 1996. *Who Is Jesus? Answers to Your Questions about the Historical Jesus.* New York: HarperCollins.

———. 2010. *The Greatest Prayer.* New York: HarperCollins.

Currivan, Jude. 2017. *The Cosmic Hologram.* Rochester, VT: Inner Traditions.

D'Angelo, Mary Rose. 1990. "Women in Luke–Acts: A Redactional View." *Journal of Biblical Literature* 109: 441–61.

———. 1999. *Women in Christian Origins.* New York: Oxford University Press.

Davidson, John. 2004. *The Secret of the Creative Vacuum.* London: C. H. Daniel.

Davies, Steven. 1995. *Jesus the Healer.* London: SCM Press.

Dawkins, Richard. 2006. *The God Delusion.* London: Bantam Books.

Day, David. 2001. *Pearl beyond Price: The Attractive Jesus.* London: Fount.

Delio, Ilia. 2013. *The Unbearable Wholeness of Being.* Maryknoll, NY: Orbis.

———. 2015. *Making All Things New.* Maryknoll, NY: Orbis.

Dennis, Trevor. 2017. *The Gospel beyond the Gospels.* London: SPCK.

Dowd, Michael. 2009. *Thank God for Evolution.* New York: Plume/Penguin.

Dunn, James G. D. 1977. *Unity and Diversity in the New Testament.* Philadelphia: Westminster Press.

———. 2003. *Christianity in the Making: Jesus Remembered.* Grand Rapids: Eerdmans.

Eldredge, N. 1999. *The Pattern of Evolution.* New York: W. H. Freeman.

Eliade, Mircea. 1964. *Shamanism: Archaic Techniques of Ecstasy.* London: Routledge & Kegan Paul.

Ettinger, Bracha. 2006. *The Matrixial Borderspace.* Minneapolis: University of Minnesota Press.

Farley, Wendy. 2011. *Gathering Those Driven Away: A Theology of Incarnation.* Louisville, KY: Westminster John Knox Press.

Feehan, John. 2012. *The Singing Heart of the World*. Dublin: Columba Press.

Fiensy, David A. 2014. *Christian Origins and the Ancient Economy*. Eugene, OR: Cascade Books.

Fowler, James. 1981. *Stages of Faith*. San Francisco: Harper & Row.

Francis. 2015. *Laudato Si': On Care for Our Common Home* [Encyclical]. Vatican: Libreria Editrice Vaticana.

Freyne, Sean. 2014. *The Jesus Movement and Its Expansion*. Grand Rapids: Eerdmans.

Fuellenbach, John. 1994. *The Kingdom of God*. Maryknoll, NY: Orbis.

Funk, Robert. 1996. *Honest to Jesus*. San Francisco: HarperSanFrancisco.

Gafney, Wilda C. 2008. *Daughters of Miriam: Women Prophets in Ancient Israel*. Minneapolis: Fortress Press.

George, Margaret. 2002. *Mary Called Magdalene*. New York: Penguin.

Girard, René. 2001. *I See Satan Fall Like Lightning*. Maryknoll, NY: Orbis Books.

Gollnick, James. 2008. *Religion and Spirituality in the Life Cycle*. New York: Peter Lang.

Grimassi, Raven. 2012. *Old World Witchcraft*. New York: Weiser.

Hall, Christine. 1996. *Order and Ministry*. Leominister: Fowler Wright Books.

Hampson, Daphne. 1996. *Swallowing a Fishbone?* London: SPCK.

Hardin, Michael. 2010. *The Jesus Driven Life*. Lancaster, PA: JDL Press.

Haskins, Susan. 1993. *Mary Magdalene: Myth and Metaphor*. New York: Harcourt Brace.

Haughey, John C. 2015. *A Biography of the Spirit*. Maryknoll, NY: Orbis Books.

Haught, John F. 2010. *Making Sense of Evolution*. Louisville, KY: Westminster John Knox Press.

———. 2015. *Resting on the Future*. New York: Bloomsbury.

———. 2017. *The New Cosmic Story*. New Haven, CT: Yale University Press.

Hawken, Paul. 2007. *Blessed Unrest*. New York: Viking.

Herzog, William. 1994. *Parables as Subversive Speech*. Louisville, KY: Westminster John Knox Press.

Hill, C. E. 2010. *Who Chose the Gospels?* Oxford: Oxford University Press.

Hillman, James. 1975. *Re-Visioning Psychology*. Washington, DC: Spring Publications.

———. 1983. *Archetypal Psychology*. Washington, DC: Spring Publications.

Horsley, Richard. 2008. *Jesus in Context: Power, People, and Performance*. Minneapolis, MN: Fortress.

———. 2012. *The Prophet Jesus and the Renewal of Israel*. Grand Rapids: Eerdmans.

———. 2014. *Jesus and Magic*. Eugene, OR: Cascade Books.

Howard-Brook, Wes. 2011. *"Come Out My People!"* Maryknoll, NY: Orbis.

———. 2016. *Empire Baptized*. Maryknoll, NY: Orbis.

Hoyle, Fred. 1950. The Nature of the Universe. Oxford (UK): Blackwell.

Hunter, Harold, and Neil Ormerod. 2013. *The Many Faces of Global Pentecostalism*. Cleveland, TN: CPT Press.

Johnson, Elizabeth. 2003. *Truly Our Sister*. New York: Continuum.

———. 2006. *Quest for the Living God*. New York: Continuum.

———. 2014. *Ask the Beasts: Darwin and the God of Love*. New York: Bloomsbury/Continuum.

———. 2018. *Creation and the Cross*. Maryknoll, NY: Orbis.

Johnson, Kurt, and David Robert Ord. 2012. *The Coming Inter-Spiritual Age*. Vancouver: Namaste Publishing.

Keller, Catherine. 2003. *The Face of the Deep*. New York: Routledge.

Kelly, Anthony J. 2015. "Human Consciousness, God and Creation." *Pacifica: Australasian Theological Studies* 28: 3–22.

Kim, Grace Ji-Sun. 2011. *The Holy Spirit, Chi, and the Other.* New York: Palgrave Macmillan.

Kim, Kirsteen. 2007. *The Holy Spirit in the World.* Maryknoll, NY: Orbis.

Kirchhoffer, David G. 2014. "Turtles All the Way Down? Pressing Questions for Theological Anthropology in the Twenty-First Century," in *Questioning the Human: Toward a Theological Anthropology for the Twenty-First Century,* edited by Lieven Boeve, Yves de Maeseneed, and Ellen Van Stichel. New York: Fordham University Press.

Knitter, Paul F. 1985. *No Other Name?* Maryknoll, NY: Orbis.

Koestler, Arthur. 1967. *The Ghost in the Machine.* New York: Penguin.

Korten, David. 2015. *Change the Story, Change the Future.* Oakland, CA: Berrett-Koehler.

Kraybill, Donald B. 1990. *The Upside-Down Kingdom.* Scottdale, PA: Herald Press.

Küng, Hans. 1974. *On Being a Christian.* London: SCM Press.

Lanzetta, Beverly. 2018. *The Monk Within: Embracing a Sacred Way of Life.* Sebastopal, CA: Blue Sapphire Books.

Lawrence, Louise J. 2013. *Sense and Stigma in the Gospels.* Oxford: Oxford University Press.

Le Grice, Keiron. 2010. *The Archetypal Cosmos.* Edinburgh: Floris Books.

Levine, Amy-Jill. 2007. *The Misunderstood Jew.* New York: HarperOne.

———. 2014. *Short Stories of Jesus.* New York: HarperOne.

Levy, Paul. 2018. *The Quantum Revelation: A Radical Synthesis of Science and Spirituality.* New York: Select Books.

Liebert, Elizabeth. 2015. *The Soul of Discernment.* Louisville, KY: Westminster John Knox Press.

Lyons, Kathleen. 2015. *Mysticism and Narcissism.* Newcastle-upon-Tyne: Cambridge Scholars.

MacKenzie, Catriona, and Natalie Stoljar. 2000. *Relational Autonomy.* New York: Oxford University Press.

Maehle, Gregor. 2012. *Pranayama: The Breath of Yoga*. Innaloo City, Australia: Kaivalya Publications.

Malone, Mary T. 2001. *Women and Christianity: The First Thousand Years*. Maryknoll, NY: Orbis.

———. 2014. *The Elephant in the Church*. Dublin: Columba Press.

Marchant, Jo. 2016. *Cure: A Journey into the Science of Mind over Body*. New York: Crown.

McCaul, T. 2007. *Yoga as Medicine*. New York: Bantam Books.

McNamara, Jo Ann Kay. 1996. *Sisters in Arms*. Cambridge, MA: Cambridge University Press.

Meier, John P. 1994. *A Marginal Jew*. Vol. 2: New Haven, CT: Yale University Press.

———. 2016. *A Marginal Jew*. Vol. 5. New Haven, CT: Yale University Press.

Meyers, Carol. 2016. *Rediscovering Eve*. New York: Oxford University Press.

Moss, Candida. 2013. *The Myth of Persecution*. New York: HarperCollins.

Neufeld, Thomas Y. 2011. *Jesus and the Subversion of Violence*. London: SPCK.

Ogden, Schubert. 1986. *On Theology*. San Francisco: Harper and Row.

Olyan, Saul. 2008. *Disability in the Hebrew Bible*. New York: Cambridge University Press.

O'Murchu, Diarmuid. 2005. *Catching Up with Jesus*. New York: Crossroad.

———. 2008. *Ancestral Grace*. Maryknoll, NY: Orbis.

———. 2010. *Adult Faith*. Maryknoll, NY: Orbis.

———. 2011. *Christianity's Dangerous Memory*. New York: Crossroad.

———. 2012. *In the Beginning Was the Spirit*. Maryknoll, NY: Orbis.

———. 2014a. *On Being a Postcolonial Christian*. North Charleston, SC: CreateSpace.

———. 2014b. *The Meaning and Practice of Faith*. Maryknoll, NY: Orbis.

————. 2017. *Incarnation: A New Evolutionary Threshold.* Maryknoll, NY: Orbis.

Osiek, Carolyn, and Margaret MacDonald. 2006. *A Woman's Place.* Minneapolis: Fortress Press.

Pagola, José Antonio. 2009. *Jesus: A Historical Approximation.* Miami, FL: Convivium Press.

Parkinson, Lorraine. 2015. *Made on Earth: How the Gospel Writers Created the Christ.* Richmond, Victoria, Australia: Spectrum.

Petroff, Elizabeth Alvilda. 1994. *Body and Soul: Essays on Medieval Women and Mysticism.* New York: Oxford University Press.

Phipps, Carter. 2012. *Evolutionaries.* New York: Harper Perennial.

Plotkin, Bill. 2008. *Nature and the Human Soul.* Novata, CA: New World Library.

Primark, Joel, and Nancy Abrams. 2006. *The View from the Center of the Universe.* New York: Riverhead Books.

Raiser, Konrad. 1991. *Ecumenism in Transition.* Geneva: WCC Publications.

Reid, Barbara. 2016. "The Gospel of Luke: Friend or Foe to Women Proclaimers of the Word?" *Catholic Biblical Quarterly* 78: 1–23.

Reid-Bowen, Paul. 2007. *Goddess as Nature.* Farnham, UK: Ashgate.

Robinson, John C. 2016. *The Divine Human.* Winchester, UK: O Books.

Rohr, Richard. 2009. *The Naked Now.* New York: Crossroad.

Rohr, Richard, with Mike Morrell. 2016. *The Divine Dance: The Trinity and Your Transformation.* New Kensington, PA: Whitaker House.

Roszak, Theodore. 1969. *The Making of a Counter Culture.* Berkeley: University of California Press.

————. 1979. *Person/Planet.* New York: Doubleday.

————. 2001. *The Longevity Revolution.* Berkeley, CA: Berkeley Hills Books.

———. 2009. *The Making of an Elder Culture*. Gabriola Island, BC: New Society Publishers.

Runesson, Anna. 2011. *Exegesis in the Making: Postcolonialism and New Testament Studies*. Leiden: Brill.

Rynne, Terence J. 2008. *Gandhi and Jesus: The Saving Power of Non-Violence*. Maryknoll, NY: Orbis.

Said, Edward. 1993. *The Politics of Dispossession*. New York: Vintage Books.

Schaberg, Jane. 2004. *The Resurrection of Mary Magdalene*. New York: Continuum.

Schafer, Lothar. 2013. *Infinite Potential: What Quantum Physics Reveals*. New York: Random House.

Schenk, Christine. 2017. *Crispina and Her Sisters*. Minneapolis: Fortress Press.

Schneiders, Sandra. 2003. *Written That You May Believe*. New York: Crossroad.

Schwager, Raymond. 1987. *Must There Be Scapegoats?* New York: Herder and Herder.

Seung, Sebastian. 2012. *Connectome: How the Brain's Wiring Makes Us How We Are*. New York: Houghton Mifflin Harcourt.

Sheehy, Gail. 1995. *Passages*. New York: Random House.

Shlain, Leonard. 1991. *Art and Physics*. New York: HarperCollins.

Siegel, Bernie. 2013. *The Art of Healing*. New World Books.

Smith, Adrian B. 1996. *The God Shift*. Winchester, UK: O Books.

Snodgrass, Klyne. 2008. *Stories with Intent*. Grand Rapids: Eerdmans.

Song, C. S. 1993. *Jesus and the Reign of God*. Minneapolis: Fortress Books.

Sorokin, Pitirim. 1950. *Modern Historical and Social Philosophies*. New York: Dover Publications.

Spong, John Shelby. 2016. *Biblical Literalism: A Gentile Heresy*. New York: HarperCollins.

Stevens, Anthony. 2002. *Archetypes: A Natural History of the Self*. London: Routledge & Kegan Paul.

Stewart, John. 2000. *Evolution's Arrow*. Canberra: Chapman Press.

Stokes, Kenneth. 1982. *Faith in the Adult Life Cycle*. New York: W. H. Sadlier.

Sullivan, Nikki. 2003. *A Critical Introduction to Queer Theory*. Edinburgh: Edinburgh University Press.

Swimme, Brian, and Thomas Berry. 1992. *The Universe Story*. New York: Penguin.

Swimme, Brian, and Evelyn Tucker. 2011. *Journey of the Universe*. New Haven, CT: Yale University Press.

Tarnas, Richard. 1991. *The Passion of the Western Mind*. New York: Random House.

———. 2006. *Cosmos and Psyche: Intimations of a New World View*. New York: Viking Penguin.

Trocmé, Andre. 2014. *Jesus and the Nonviolent Revolution*. New York: Plough Publishing House.

Twelftree, Graham. 1999. *Jesus the Miracle Worker*. Downers Grove, IL: InterVarsity Press.

Wallace, Marc I. 2003. *Fragments of the Spirit*. Harrisburg, PA: Trinity Press International.

———. 2005. *Finding God in the Singing River*. Minneapolis: Fortress.

Welker, Michael, ed. 2006. *The Work of the Spirit*. Grand Rapids: Eerdmans.

Wilber, Ken, Dick Anthony, and Bruce Ecker. 1987. *Spiritual Choices: The Problem of Recognizing Authentic Paths to Inner Transformation*. New York: Paragon House.

Wink, Walter. 1992. *Engaging the Powers*. Minneapolis: Fortress.

———. 2002. *The Human Being: Jesus and the Enigma of the Son of Man*. Minneapolis: Augsburg Fortress.

Winter, Miriam Therese. 2009. *Paradoxology: Spirituality in a Quantum Universe*. Maryknoll, NY: Orbis.

Zimmermann, Ruben. 2015. *Puzzling the Parables of Jesus*. Minneapolis: Fortress.

Znamenski, Andrei. 2007. *The Beauty of the Primitive*. New York: Oxford University Press.

Index